**REI Editions**

All of our ebooks can be read on the following devices:
- Computer
- eReaders
- iOS
- Android
- Blackberries
- Windows
- Tablet
- Cellular

**French Academy**

**Chiromancy**

ISBN: 9782372974837

Published: January 2023
New edition completely revised and updated: March 2025
Copyright © 2023 - 2025 R.E.I. Editions
www.rei-editions.com

French Academy

# Chiromancy

R.E.I. Editions

# Book Index

**Chiromancy**

Chiromancy is the art of describing the personality and predicting the fate of an individual through the study of the palm of his hand. The word comes from the Greek "cheiromantéia", composed of "chéir", hand and "mantéia", divination.

The practice, widespread throughout the world, albeit with numerous cultural variations, is also known as palm reading; the chiromancy practitioner is called a palmist, chirologist, or hand reader.

Chiromancy, universally considered a pseudoscience, is divided into two main disciplines:
- Chirology, which deals with the study of the palm lines.
- Chirognomy, which deals with the study of the shape of the hand.

Chiromancy has its origins in Indian astrology of which it was a discipline; the Hindu sage Valmiki would be credited with a book now lost, the title of which could be translated as "The teachings of Maharishi Valmiki on male palmistry".

This book would have contained 567 stanzas and may have been written more than 5,000 years ago.

From India, the art of palm reading then spread to China around 3000 BC; subsequently it reached Tibet, Egypt, Persia and developed in Greece, where it was also practiced by the philosopher Anaxagoras.

Indian chiromancy claims to be the oldest, but it is mostly transmitted verbally, through a process known as "parampara", within family, social and cultural groups.

In India, palm reading is an integral part of most natural medicine practices.

Palm reading is also part of the Indian version of astrology, known as jyotish; it is quite common for Indian Ayurvedic practitioners to be skilled in palmistry. Indian chiromancy is more predictive than Western palmistry which is holistic and focuses more on psychological qualities.

Chinese chiromancy is said to be about 3,000 years old and part of the original traditional Chinese medicine; in China, palmistry is known as shou xiang and shou zhen. Chinese chiromancy uses its own terms to define parts of the hand, referring instead to lines based on elements or mounts based on certain stars, rather than planets.

Chinese chiromancy has three different systems based on trigrams, stars or lines. The Chinese trigram system is based on the bagua map, which is also used in feng shui, and has clear and direct links to different organs and systems within the body. An ancient Chinese belief believes that each finger corresponds to someone dear to us:

- The little finger represents the children.
- The middle finger represents ourselves.
- The thumb represents the parents.
- The index finger represents brothers and sisters.
- The ring finger represents the partner.

The development in the classical era has left traces in the terminology, which indicates some parts of the palm and hand using the names of the ancient Greek and Roman gods.

Chiromancy, named after the famous palmist Count Louis Hamon, also known as Cheiro, is a very popular and accurate type of divination; from the scant information we have about Celtic Europe, there is reason to believe that here too the hand was considered a source of information about the person.

The hand changes throughout existence; the lines we see on our palm now weren't the same a year ago and will likely be very different five years from now; although the hand provides an outline of life, it is only generic.

Palmistry also spread through Roma and other Gypsy peoples, who traditionally still practice it. To date, no satisfactory research has yet been conducted either in support or in contrast to the scientific nature of this practice, which is generally considered a pseudoscience, like astrology and cartomancy.

- This is due to its total lack of scientific foundation and possibility of verification.

There are many different interpretations of hand lines in different schools of palmistry, and modern palmists often combine traditional fortune-telling techniques with psychology, holistic medicine, and other methods of divination.

- The complete reading should not be done only with the palm.

The hand, like the foot, contains all the information concerning the life of the person, so it must be studied in its entirety, the lines, the palm, the back, the fingers, the nails, and NOT just the left hand, typically gypsy like method, but both hands, since:

- The left is what will be. Not only that, the palm of the left hand reveals the predispositions, the gifts we receive even before birth. If the lines of the left hand are more marked than those of the right, it means that we have not fully exploited our abilities and that we have more possibilities than we ourselves believe, but we have let ourselves be hindered by the passive nature, by adverse conditions, by laziness. This is characteristic of misunderstood geniuses, of unknown poets and of the resigned.

- The right is what it is and has been. The palm of the right hand therefore records the use that we have made and continue to make of these qualities. If it is the right hand that has the most marked lines then the hands belong to stubborn, resolute, brutal and careerist individuals.

If the lines are almost equal in the two hands, the subjects are peaceful, but without strength of character and little personality. In left-handed situations previously listed, of course, are reversed.

In women and men the situation is different:

W omen have the right hand which represents the status in which they came into the world, while the left hand tells us about all the life experiences accumulated over the years and which have acted to change the cultural baggage with which we were born .

- In humans it is quite the opposite: the left hand will be the "speaking" one at the moment of birth, while the right will represent all the experiences made during one's life.

Some currents of thought argue that it is the left hand that shows the future, but with a probability rather than an absolute certainty.

If the person whose hands you are observing shows a difference between the two palms, this could mean that he has taken or is taking actions to change the potential of his life.

The size of the hands offers a first indication of the character. The length of the hand corresponds to approximately one tenth of the person's height, as well as the distance from the chin to the hairline, or a little less.

- Very small hands signal great sensitivity, as well as cheerfulness, inconstancy and imagination.
- Very large hands indicate poor sensitivity and analytical intelligence, as well as slow instinctive reactions.
- The long and large hand is a sign of selfishness and a strong ability to impose one's will on others.

- Large hands with short arms are associated with great aggression.
- The well-proportioned hand, compared to the size of the body, indicates a balanced, honest, judicious and discreet person; this hand, opening, forms a straight line with its fingers.

Color, temperature and humidity of the hand reveal the psycho-physical conditions of the subject.

- Rosy hands show affection and happiness.
- Reddish hands both optimism and anger.
- Very pale or yellowish hands. Nervousness, low energy and inner closure.

In the back , joint flexibility, skin texture and hairiness reveal important characteristics.

- Stiff hands can show both resoluteness and energy as well as clumsiness and shyness.
- Flexible hands show adaptability.
- Soft and soft hands indicate the weak character of someone who is easily influenced.
- Hands with rough skin express practical sense .
- Hands with fine skin indicate delicacy in feelings.

For the value to be given to the signs it is important to recognize the prevailing hand which, commonly understood, is the one most used both for writing and in the various activities in which the hand is involved.

- In doubtful cases, the automatic crossing of the thumbs while bringing the hands together helps determine which is the prevailing hand for chirology: the thumb of the prevailing hand is always placed on top of the other.

The left hand expresses our most feminine part, our affectivity, sensitivity, imagination and aesthetic sense, while the right hand expresses the masculine part, logical thinking, rationality and active behavior.

- In case of left hand prevalence, we have a lively imagination and little adaptability to social conventions.
- If the prevalence is in the right hand, we find rationality and conformity.

The prevailing hand often has a greater number of lines than the other and it is important to define how these lines differed, or in any case are different, from those of the non-prevailing hand, which is considered less changeable.

- The prevailing (most used) hand tends to show the aspects of our character that are more easily expressed in everyday life.
- The non -prevailing (less used) hand reveals our innate characteristics, the latent and unexpressed qualities, the parts of us that we like least and that we have tried to change.

In the non-main hand the lines (and their endings) remain almost unchanged over the years and show the innate characteristics, while in the main hand they deviate from the model still present in the other hand, thus expressing the acquired characteristics.

The gestures and mimicry that accompany, reinforce and often replace words, manifest what the Latins called "oratory gesture": indispensable in social relationships, our hands guide, threaten and bless, they know how to caress and hit, they express us in work by handling with equal skill the farmer's spade and the surgeon's scalpel, the blacksmith's hammer and the artist's brush, speak for the dumb and read for the blind; all of this is part of daily practice, it is an acquired and taken for granted fact for everyone.

However, there are other languages that we neglect, or even ignore, that hands generously offer us; let's observe its shape, the relationship between the palm and the fingers, the relationship between the fingers: we will be able to derive our basic characteristics from it, the rigid armor within which we can move, the immutable aspects of the personality, as it remains immutable during throughout life the structure of the hand that grows with us while keeping its proportions fixed.

- According to the " Theory of the three worlds" , we will know if we are more instinctive than rational or if emotions direct our choices.

The comparison between the left and right hand highlights any contradictions and how much we waste, or use well, the natural potential.

Then there is the dynamic aspect, the language of our growth which in the swelling of the mountains tells us how much energy we are supplied with, in the shape and changing development of the lines it speaks to us of emotions and rationality, vitality and the relationship we manage to build with those around us, lines that mark the future path in its most important and crucial moments.

Finally, there are the "particular signs", the most whimsical and personal element, which help to photograph the present situation in the most intimate details.

The two hands are the poles of life through which our existence develops, the symbol of the beginning and of the realization, they unite feminine and masculine in a single total being; for this both must be observed, as they both compose and represent us with very distinct and defined meanings, and only from their union can the entire personality be derived.

From their comparison it is possible to draw interesting tests on the use we make of our abilities, if and how much we are wasting what intimately belongs to us, how educational and cultural conditioning and ephemeral fads act on us.

Let us look at the three possible cases .

- The left has more lines - The meaning is very precise: our life is marked by renunciations, and we are betraying some more intimate aspirations, a situation that requires a pause for reflection.

  If the line of destiny is missing on the right, which is instead very clear on the left, the problem is linked to study or work whose choice was not the happiest, either because it was imposed by others, or by contingent needs, or from anything else: the road is not the right one, and maybe it's time to change course.

  If then from the left mount of Venus come numerous lines that cut that of life and which do not find correspondence on the right, it is our emotions that suffer because they cannot find an outlet towards the outside: fear, shyness, insecurity, let's look in the mirror .

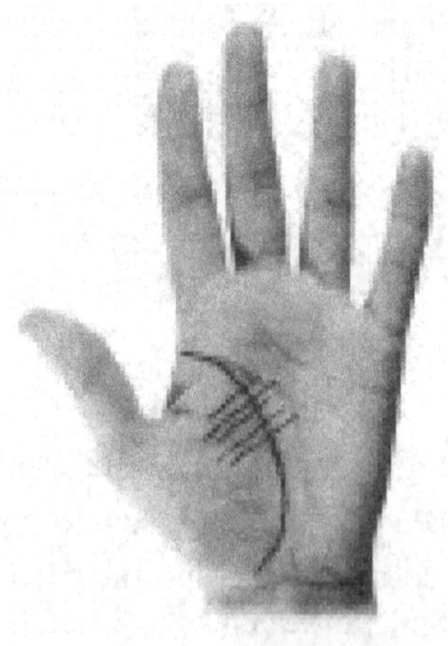

- When the lines appear more numerous on the right palm, it is ambition that dominates, together with the desire for power that we seek to realize in all our actions.
  Only reality has value and only what is objective and tangible has meaning.
  It is a situation that can create coldness and aridity.

- The rarest case of a good balance between the two hands that have similar lines, indicates that the lucky owner is following the right path and will be able to unwind the thread of his existence with a few simple knots.

**Theory of the three worlds**

It is a fascinating theory that emerges from the mists of time, never denied over the centuries, and which has always accompanied every method of investigation into the human personality that this doctrine has on three levels: the natural-instinctive one, the rational-psychic one that of spiritual communication.
This triple subdivision is proposed on the hand that presents:
 In the lowest part of the palm, near the wrist up to the line of the head, the " Corpus ", the expression of the deepest instincts.
- The other half of the palm, up to the joint of the fingers, is the " Animus " which speaks to us of the extent of ambitions and the need for social affirmation.
- Finally, the fingers measure the " Spiritus ", that is sensitivity, refinement, spirituality.

Which of the three parts appears more evident at first glance:
- If it's the first, the Corpus, then we tend to be impulsive and instinct easily gets carried away.
- If it is the Animus, we are the concrete and rational ones who analyze every action.
- If the fingers are the longest part, then the approach to life is based on spiritual communication.

Let us now observe the fingers which, in the segments that compose them, reproduce the subdivision of the three worlds.

- If the first phalanx, the one joined to the palm, is the most robust and evident, then we are enjoyers linked to the pleasures that life offers and to which we casually give in.

- If the second, central one is the most evident, then we are serious, studious and reflective.
- If the longest is the external one, then idealism and spirituality are the emotions we tend to get lost in.

We can have a further verification by observing the three main lines that run through the entire palm of the hand, marking our journey from beginning to end with its joys and its pains.

- The Life Line, which surrounds the base of the thumb, expresses vitality and survival instinct.
- The Line of the Head, which starts from the same point between the thumb and forefinger, shows the ability to understand and the quality of psychic tension.
- The Line of the Heart, which starts from the opposite side of the hand, under the little finger, and communicates the emotion and affection we are provided with.

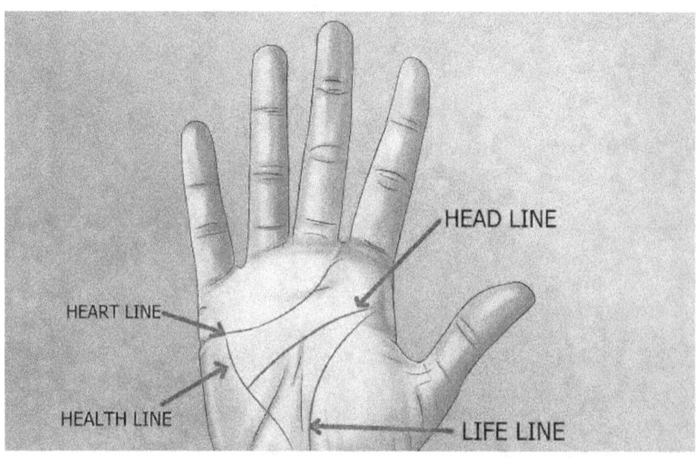

**The shape of the hand**

The various combinations of the shape of the palm and fingers define the type of hand according to the study of so-called chirognomy.
A first classification distinguishes four types, linked to the elements of astrology.
1. Hand of Earth or Practice.
2. Hand of Fire or Creative.
3. Hand of Air or Intellectual.
4. Hand of Water or Sensitive.

**Hand of Earth**

His palm is broad and square with short, rather squat fingers and compact muscles; palms and fingers square, skin thick or rough and reddish in color: palms equal in length to fingers.

- Solid values and energy, sometimes stubborn.
- Practical and responsible, sometimes materialistic.
- Works with hands, comfortable with material activities.
- From an aesthetic point of view it is not among the most beautiful, but it is certainly the most reliable because it is typical of responsible, concrete and loyal individuals, qualities that we would like to find in best friends.

People of this type have practical sense and organizational skills, are hardworking and resistant and never back down when it's time to roll up their sleeves for themselves and for others.

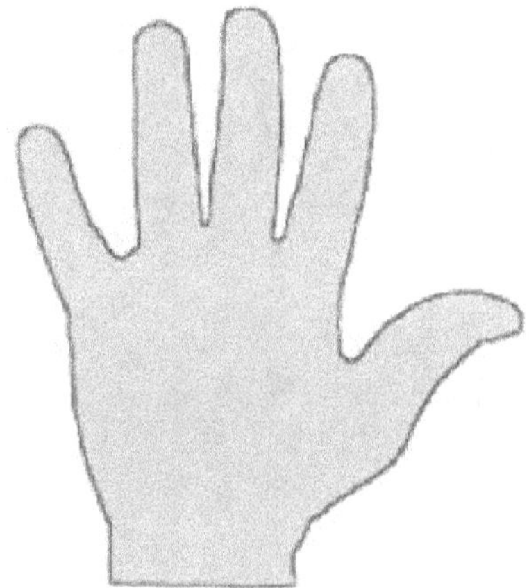

They love the outdoors and nature.

- The lines, few and well marked, reinforce the sense of clarity and essentiality.

As defects it can be said that, at times, they are a little impatient, and the considerable energy charge with which they are provided can explode in sudden anger, but don't worry, it passes immediately without aftermath and rancor.

**Hand of Fire**

The palm is long with the fingers proportionally short. Square or rectangular palms, pink or reddish skin, short fingers: length of the palms much greater than that of the fingers.

- Spontaneous, enthusiastic and optimistic.
- Sometimes selfish, impulsive and insensitive.
- Outgoing.
- He acts boldly and instinctively.
- It belongs to the enthusiastic person full of vitality who puts great passion into all the initiatives he undertakes, an often contagious passion which automatically transforms him into an inspiring leader.

He loves the unexpected, novelties and risks with the same unconscious freshness of a child.

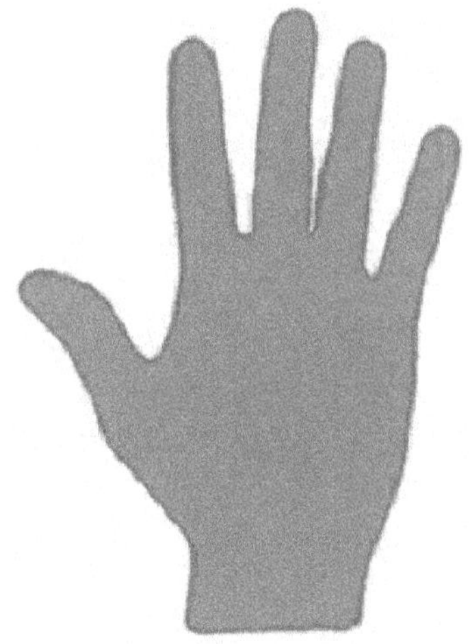

The eclecticism and dynamism are also reinforced by the numerous and well-defined lines.

As defects we can say that, sometimes, she can't finish what she starts because it's often too much even for her, and the rapid enthusiasm sometimes turns into as many rapid falls, but she immediately finds a good reason to get up.

**Hand of Air**

The palm is square with very long, lively fingers and numerous fine lines; long fingers and sometimes protruding knuckles, low-set thumbs and dry skin: palms shorter than fingers.

- Sociable, talkative and sharp.
- He can be superficial, spiteful and cold.
- Comfortable with everything mental and intangible.
- It acts in different and extremist ways.
- It belongs to the extroverted, sociable and thoughtful person with the gift of easy communication.

Her curious, penetrating and acute intelligence makes her a skilled investigator in the constant search for new intellectual and cultural stimuli.

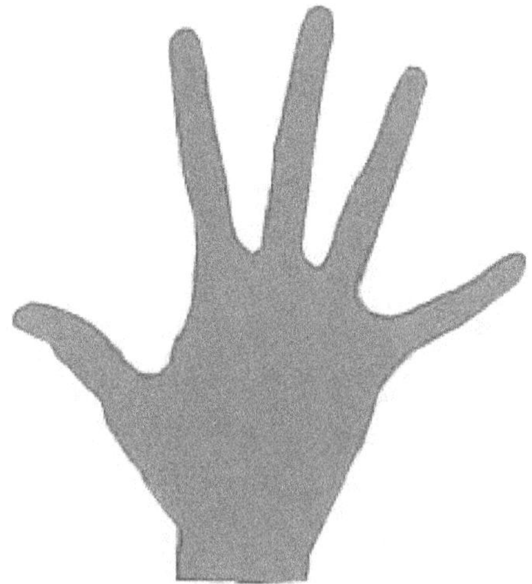

Equipped with good listening and understanding skills, she tends to take charge of, and often solve, the problems of others. As defects it can be said that giving too much value to intelligence sometimes leads it to neglect the importance of intuitions and emotions and to fall into arid intellectualism.

**Hand of Water**

With a fragile and delicate appearance, thin and tapered both in the palm and in the long fingers, it is the most elegant shape: length of the palms equal to that of the fingers, but smaller width.

- Creative, intuitive and understanding.
- Can be moody, emotional and inhibited.
- Introvert.
- He acts calmly and intuitively.
- The main characteristic that she expresses is her strong sensitivity and she is endowed with a personality full of creativity and imagination.

Its owners love to live in dreams and in the inner life and their intuition leads them to perceive the details of situations.

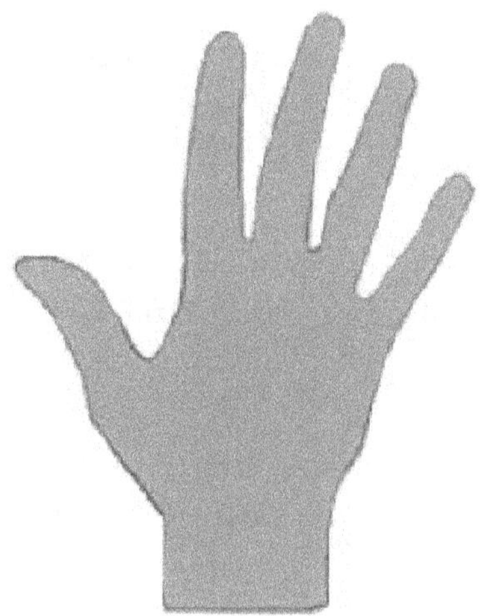

The thin, numerous and often confused lines testify to an intense emotional life.

As defects it can be said that living in fantasy often leads them to detach from reality and isolation, and daily obligations make them subject to continuous mood swings that give the impression of ambiguity.

- Two down-to-earth people can have a solid, lasting and happy union, perhaps a little too down-to-earth and without great flights, but indestructible.

- The relationship between land and water is ideal: they compensate and enrich each other with reality and fantasy, resulting in a happy and stimulating union for both.

- Very positive between the air type and the fire type: excellent combination between idea and action, stimulus and realization.

- Living in their own world, two aqua types risk dreaming together but never meeting, unless they manage to enter the same dream.

- The relationship between two fire-types that both tend to command is difficult: too many lightning strikes for a long peaceful coexistence.

- The union between two types of air is also risky, valid on an intellectual level, but one does not live on ideas alone.

- The sentimental relationship between the land and air types is risky, more functional in the business relationship between those who produce and those who sell.

- The relationship between the type of water and fire can end in two ways: either the water puts out the fire, or the fire boils the water until not even a drop remains, therefore, in any case, short-lived.

- The union between the water type and the air type is incompatible, just as emotions and reason are intolerant of each other, speaking two different languages: risk of total incommunicability.

**Hands and Planets**

An interesting classification concerns the combination of hands with planets, so we will have:

- Hand of Mars
- Hand of Venus
- Hand of Mercury
- Hand of the Moon
- Hand of the Sun
- Hand of the Virgin
- Hand of Libra
- Hand of Pluto
- Hand of Jupiter
- Hand of Saturn
- Hand of Uranus
- Hand of Neptune

**Hand of Mars**

It is the fighting hand which, in its square and robust shape, expresses power and action.
The lines, few and well defined, indicate simple objectives, well targeted and, when the two mountains of Mars are evident, of sure execution.

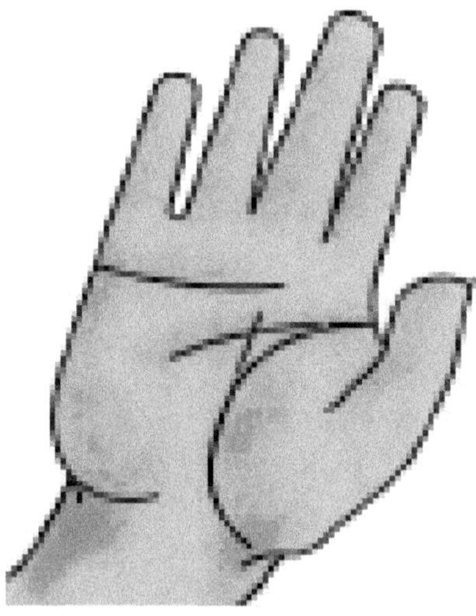

- Positive Mount of Mars - Located between that of Venus and Jupiter, it expresses courage and fighting ability that become aggression when it is too swollen. If it is flat, reticence and a defensive attitude prevail.

- Mount of Mars negative - Located between the mount of Mercury and that of the Moon, it represents fortitude, tenacity and the ability to resist pressure. If it is missing, perseverance and certainty of convictions are scarce.

Concreteness, the strong point of this hand, however becomes its limit when it tends to reject everything that goes beyond reality.

Of few nuances, he is quick in his judgments, impetuous and passionate in his affections, generous and faithful in his friendships, reliable in his work.

**Hand of Venus**

It finds its centrality on the mount at the base of the thumb which must be broad and consistent.
At first glance it appears as the most evident part of the hand which, conical in shape, tends to narrow as it rises towards the fingers.

- It reveals an affectionate temperament, driven by sentimentality and full of natural charm.

If it is too charged and hard and the energy cannot find an outlet, it can lead to perversions of a sexual nature.
When the phalanges of the fingers are plump at the bases and have dimples on the dorsal side, then we are faced with a sensual and greedy pleasure-seeker.

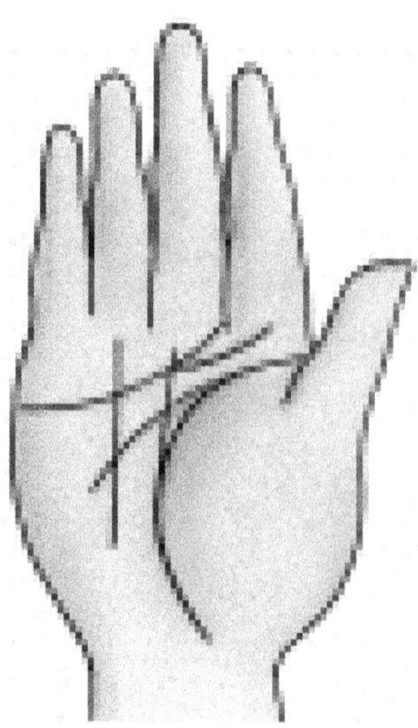

**Hand of Mercury**

The most evident characteristic of this hand lies in the short and thin fingers, very lively, agile and mobile.
Expresses the ability to make quick decisions even if sometimes it is superficial.

- Its owners have a curious, outgoing, open-minded personality to the point of being, at times, not very reliable.

The central finger is the little finger, of Mercury, which often appears detached and independent from the others, thus signaling the free thinker.
When the mount at its base is very pronounced, the subject has good speaking qualities; if a triangle then appears, financial success will not be lacking.

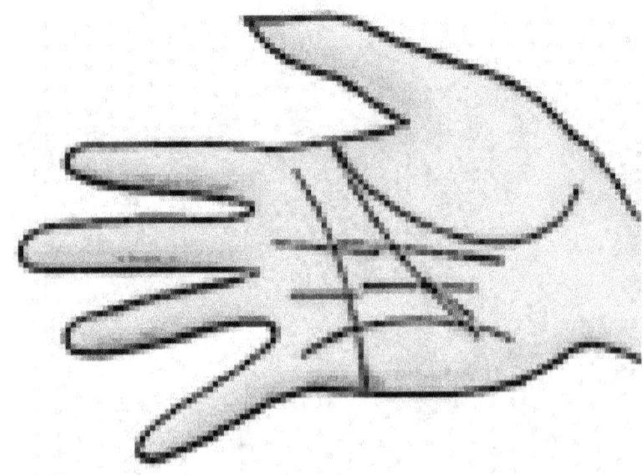

**Hand of the Moon**

It looks long and narrow, supple and delicate with numerous fine and intricate lines.

- It is the dreaming hand, brought more to contemplation than to action (not for nothing in Renaissance paintings does it belong to saints and ascetics), beautiful to look at, but impractical and unsuitable for manual work.

Their owners tend more to adapt to reality rather than modify it. How much the dream can become concrete is verified on the Monte della Luna, the true central expression of this type of hand: when it appears evident, pointed and well marked, then the fantasy becomes reality, otherwise the dreams remain in the drawer.

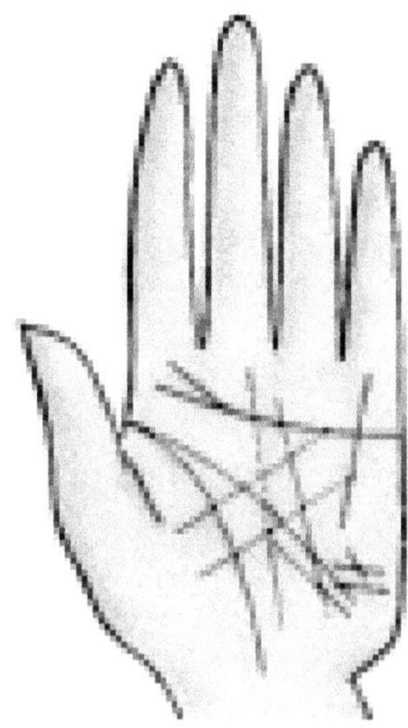

**Hand of the Sun**

It is the hand that finds its central axis in the ring finger, Apollo's finger, which must be longer than the index.

- It expresses creativity, love for art and beauty through an inner search.

If it is almost as long as the middle finger, introspection becomes obsessive, an end in itself and risks plunging the subject into a black hole from which it is difficult to get out with consequent problems of a psychic nature.
A star on the mountain below indicates that intimate satisfaction is close at hand and, for those who realize themselves in art, concrete success as well.

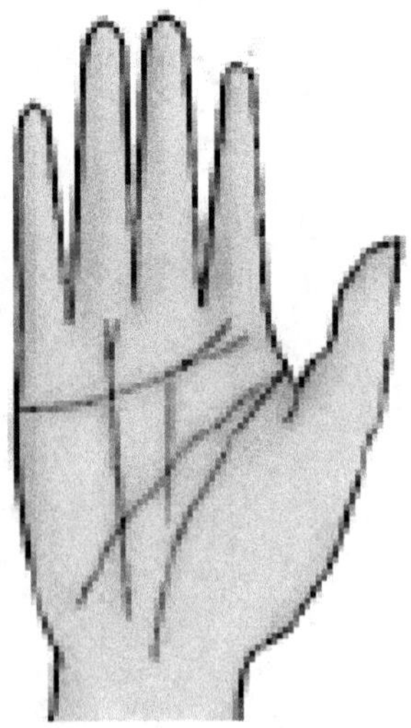

**Hand of Pluto**

Square in shape, with strong and long fingers and well highlighted mountains, an important characteristic which gives the subject the ability to always find within himself the energy to do and start over.

It is, in fact, led to continuous renewal, and the changes are evident on the fragmented line of destiny which leaves the previous experience behind in every section.

- However, the most personal notes are found in the line of intuition which, by bringing the mysteries of the unconscious and invisible to the outside, makes it enigmatic and fascinating.

The possible lascivious line (indicated by the arrow), often present on both hands, also reveals the search for strong emotions and sensations.

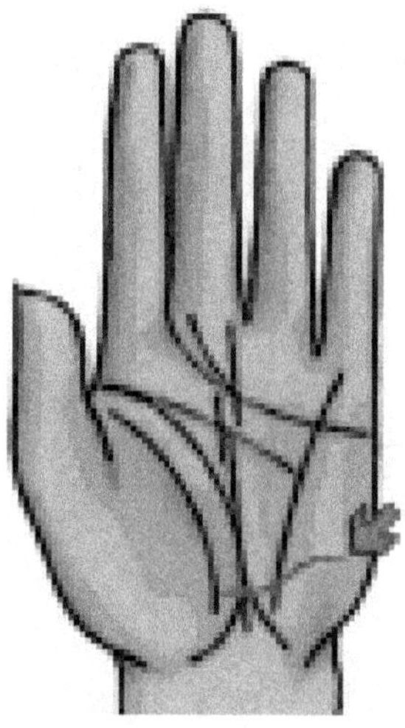

Its limit lies in the difficulty of finding the limit, and when the mountains are too full and the lines are deep and red, then creativity can turn into histrionics, perceptions into anguish, the need for novelty into self-destruction.

**Hand of Jupiter**

It finds its strong point in the index longer than the ring finger and which tends to detach from the other fingers.

- It is the finger of Jupiter, which imposes and threatens but also indicates the way; from this type of hand the ability to command, to organize and direct, and to its owner a strong drive for self-assertion.

If in its extension it reaches the middle finger, then the positive qualities turn into excesses, and authoritarianism, pride and will to power (it is not for nothing that it is also called Napoleon's finger) predominate.
A triangle on the mountain at its base legitimizes organizational and managerial ability while a square addresses these abilities to the field of teaching.

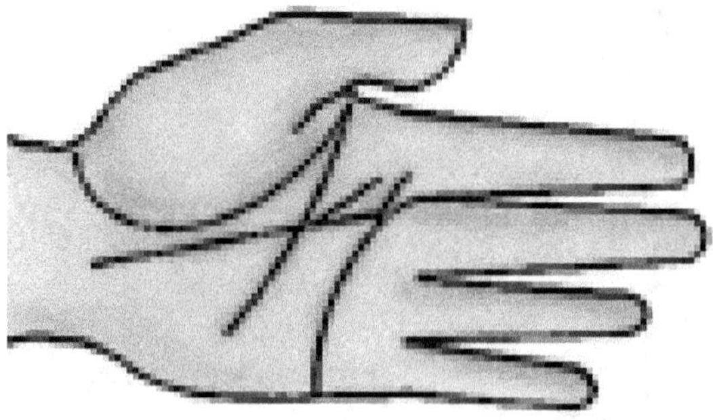

## Hand of Saturn

Long, thin fingers with knobbly joints are the hallmarks of this type of hand.

- We are faced with the serious, thoughtful person who loves to study, methodical and tenacious on whose reliability we can count.

When the middle finger, Saturn's finger, is too long, introversion, detachment and proud isolation from others are accentuated; when the index and ring fingers bend towards him then the serious person becomes conventional, conformist and conservative.

A cross on the mountain below indicates a period of pessimism and depression which can also cause physical health problems.

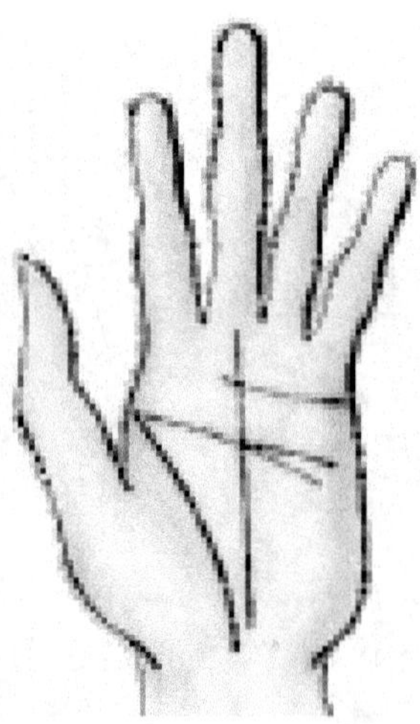

**Hand of Uranus**

It is the hand in the shape of an inverted trapezoid with the palm widening going up from the wrist to the junction of the fingers.

- It expresses the type of activity, which lives in continuous effort, often restless and dissatisfied with the situation it is experiencing, projected forward.

When the fingertips are spatulate, i.e. spread out towards the outer end, the subject often falls into a frenzy of doing, to the point of undertaking new initiatives without having completed the previous ones.
Then the nervous energy that sustains activism becomes restlessness that is transmitted to others causing reactions of annoyance and intolerance.

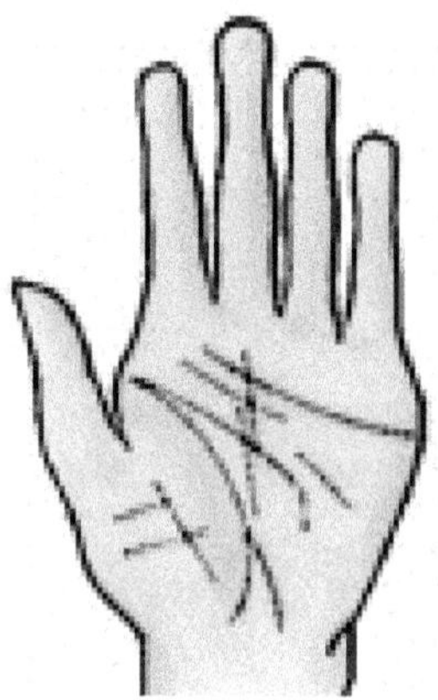

## Hand of Neptune

It belongs to the aqua hand type and as such it appears narrow and long, but with the mount of Venus very evident, numerous lines and above all a lively dynamic of particular signs.

- It is the hand that expresses, through extreme contradictions and radical metamorphoses, the restlessness of the soul.

From mystical moments and high philosophical and spiritual drives, its owner passes to interests of pure materialism, often exasperated by the presence of the lascivious line (indicated by the arrow) and also treated at a low level, while from phases of acute and elevated creativity it often falls in introversion and in the blackest apathy.
His mediumistic abilities are among the highest and in his intense moments the mount of the moon is colored in a deep pink.

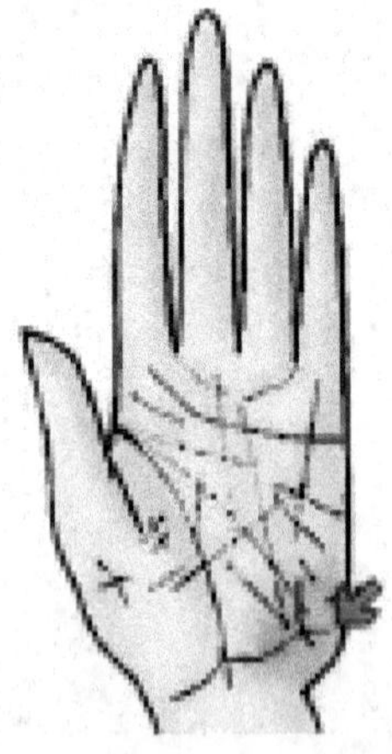

## The mountains

The mountains correspond to the fleshy parts of the hand and each one is made to correspond to a planet, including the Sun and the Moon, which, although not such, were considered in ancient times on a par with the others (today we know that the Sun is a star and that the Moon is a satellite).

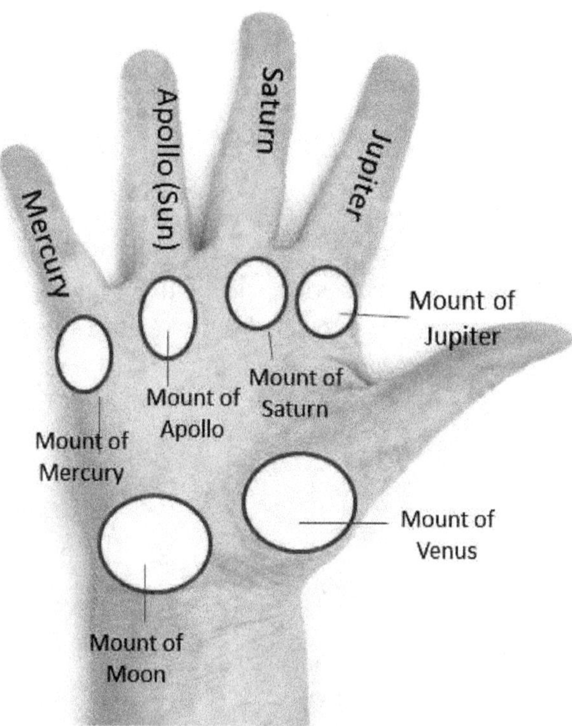


The Mountains reveal the psychophysical state, the sensuality and the natural inclinations of the person.
Their prominence indicates that certain attitudes and properties are balanced, positive and well expressed.

When the mountain is , on the other hand, depressed, i.e. it is not pronounced, it is an indication of dispersion of energy and a decrease in vitality.

When overdeveloped, it denotes imbalance and disharmony of the peculiarities attributed to the mountain. When it is more prominent than the others, it means that the qualities corresponding to that mount prevail over the others.

If the mountain tends to move to the nearby one, it means that there is a fusion of the qualities of these two. When the mounts are slightly prominent or even absent, they indicate that the qualities corresponding to the mount are manifested in a negative sense.

- The mount can be more or less developed, but also flat.

Obviously "in medio stat virtus" that is if the mountain is flat it means that there is a lack of certain characteristics in the person, if too developed the characteristics tend to exaggerate and, therefore, to become negative, so the hand of a good personality provides for medium-developed mountains.

**Mount of the Moon**

Monte della Luna is linked to imagination, intuition and mystery; it is located in the lower part of the hand, opposite the mount of Venus, near the junction of the wrist.
The scientific name is hypothenar eminence.
Indicates the consultant's aptitude for love and friendship , any restlessness of the soul and fickleness.

- If flat it is rigid it denotes a lack of inclination to love.
- If pronounced it indicates a person full of charisma, altruism, who lives to love and to be loved.

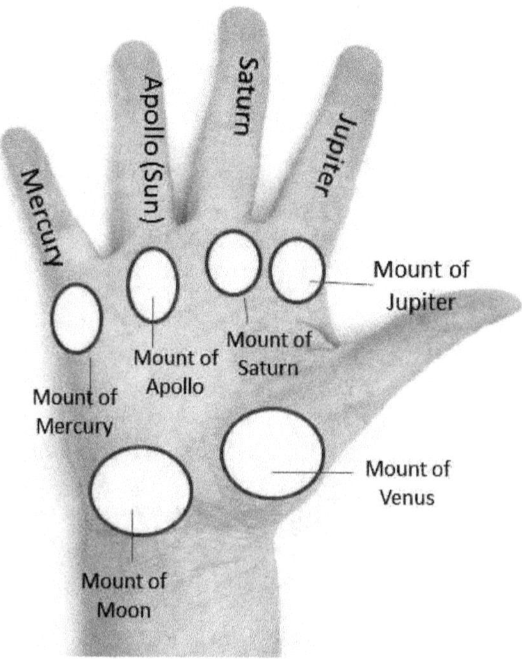


A grid on the Mount of the Moon indicates melancholy or shallowness, selfishness and lack of sensitivity.

A star placed on a transversal line indicates that in life the consultant will make or has already made a sea voyage.
A cross indicates an imaginative person who tends to escape from the real world.

**The Mount of Mercury**

The Mount of Mercury represents wisdom and the ability to think.
It is located at the base of the little finger.

- If it is pronounced and clearly visible, it indicates that the consultant is suitable for commerce, medical and scientific activities as well as all professions that require ease of speech.
- If flat and rigid in shape it indicates the opposite.
- If it is completely missing, these skills may be very limited and/or in any case not genuine.

A star or even a cross on the mount of Mercury is an indication of attachment to material goods.

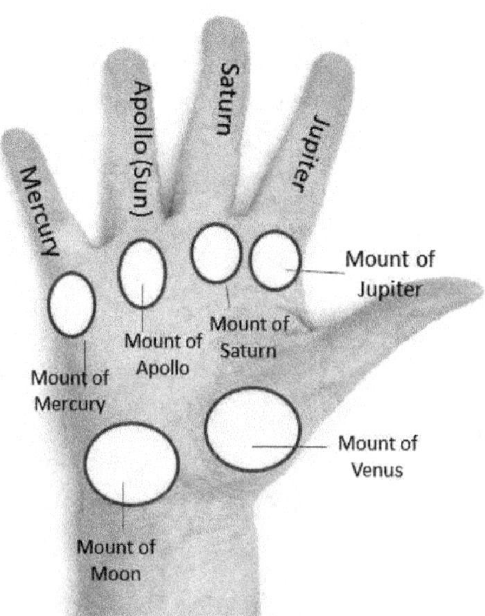

## The Mount of Apollo

The Mount of Apollo is mainly related to emotion, interest, wealth and vision of beauty.

Positioned at the base of the ring road, it is also known as Monte del Sole, it determines the propensity to taste and sensitivity , it is the world of creatives, artists and poets.

- If flat and rigid, it indicates the failure to realize one's artistic aspirations.
- If pronounced and soft, the fullness of one's artistic and professional realization. Financially, one is led to seek results in the business world and a sentimental relationship with wealthy people is preferred.
- Overdevelopment indicates an exhibitionist personality for which glory and admiration are paramount.

A star or a clear triangle on Mount Apollo indicate success, a disharmonious line indicates that the consultant is guilty of excessive exhibitionism, a grid, however, indicates the presence of obstacles.

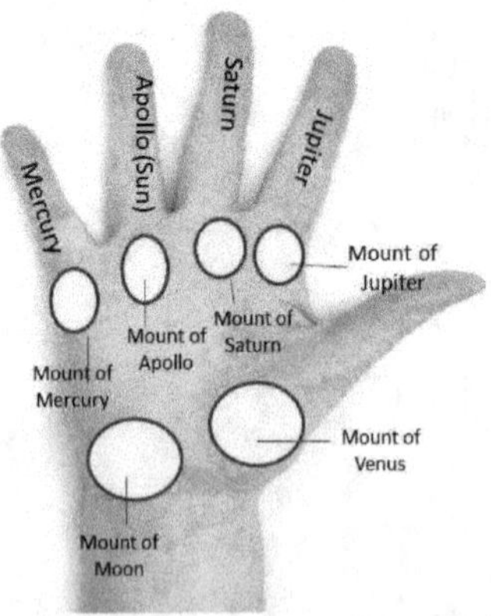

## The Mount of Saturn

The Mount of Saturn is related to the wholeness and perspective of things. It is located at the root of the middle finger, it is also called Monte del Destino, it indicates the moral sense and the propensity for business .

- If the relief of the mountain is evident , it indicates a strong moral sense and a good aptitude for business.
- If the mount is stiff and flat it indicates exactly the opposite.
- In the case of a sinking , it means that the consultant is endowed with a strong spirituality.

A cross on the mount of Saturn indicates mysticism and natural predisposition for all that is esoteric.

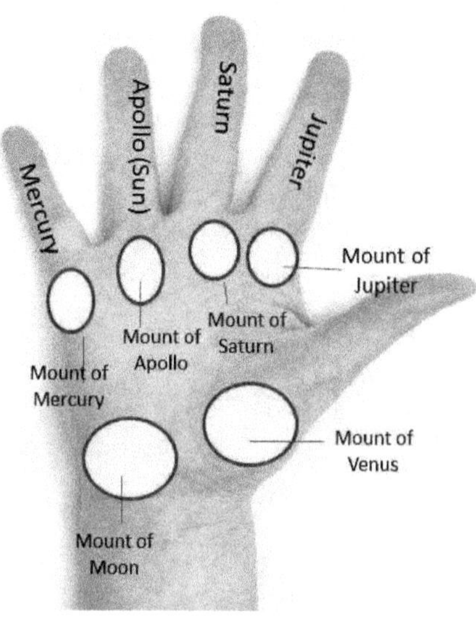

## The Mount of Jupiter

The Mount of Jupiter is a symbol of willpower, authority, ambition and self-respect.

It is placed at the base of the index and reveals the reactions we have towards the outside world; in astrology Jupiter is the "great Beneficent", brings good luck and success in life.

- If pronounced and soft, it reflects a strong personality, with a predisposition for important roles.
- If overdeveloped, however, it indicates an inordinate desire for success and a thirst for power.
- If flat and rigid, it reflects a strong practical sense.

A cross of St. Andrew on the Mount of Jupiter communicates to the palmist that there is a marriage crowned with love or a successful union.

A symbology similar to the Y indicates the end of a marriage.

A grid indicates obstacles, difficulties in achieving one's ambitions.

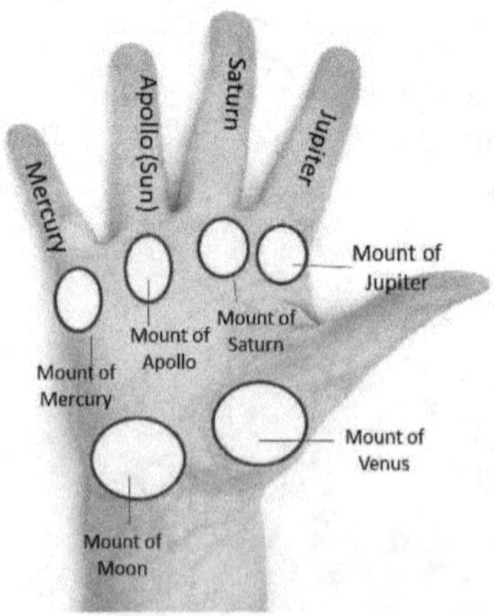

**The Mount of Venus**

The Mount of Venus is mainly related to love, health and affection.

It is located at the base of the thumb, the scientific name is thenar eminence.

It is known as the mountain of vitality which it effectively expresses in the broadest sense of the term: in fact, it reflects vigor, enthusiasm for life, sexual energy.

- The more the mount is swollen and pinkish , the greater these qualities can be.
- If the area is really highly developed, the person will show an exaggerated desire for attention and affection, as well as a huge self-centeredness.
- A low and flattened mountain expresses a more tranquil love, a tendency to reserve and sometimes coldness.

The presence of lines on this mountain indicate the sufferings experienced, a grid denotes inconstancy in love and a strong tendency towards infidelity.

A star , located almost at the base of the thumb, reveals difficult love.

A cross highlights an overwhelming love that will affect the whole life, if this line is well defined and clear; if the crosses are more than one, the loves will be equally numerous. Also, the lower the cross is, the older the love in question will be.

If present a triangle denounces superficiality in love and disorder in emotional life.

- The valley of Neptune is a depression, which clearly separates the mounts of Venus and the Moon.

It manifests the charisma with which we can be endowed, that is, that extraordinary power of guidance and persuasion that some people have, capable of offering themselves as a model, for the trust and admiration they manage to arouse among the people.

These characteristics are present when, with a thumb pressure on the affected parts, they barely whiten, to immediately become compact again.

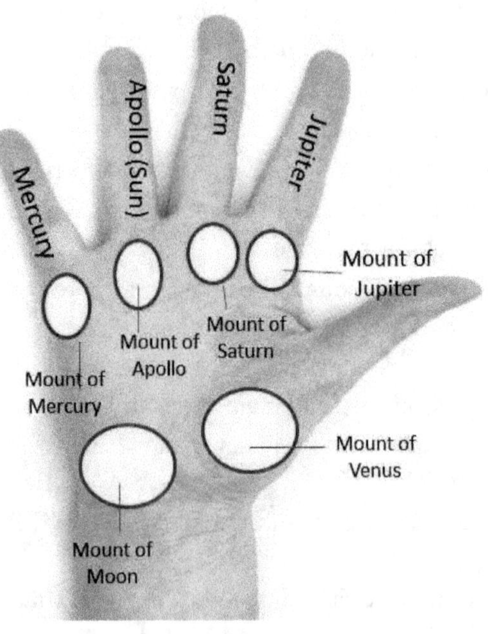

**The Mount of Mars**

The mountain dedicated to the god of War is divided into Internal or Positive Mars (between the mount of Venus and Jupiter), External or Negative Mars (between the mount of the Moon and Mercury) and Piana di Marte (in the center between the other two).

- **Inner Mount of Mars**

Located between that of Venus and Jupiter, it expresses courage and fighting ability that become aggression when it is too swollen. It is also called Mars Minor / Inferior or Mars Positive and is therefore linked to courage and adventure.
  - If this mount is well developed and prominent, it indicates a very brave, healthy and adventurous person. Many famous soldiers and generals usually have this type of conformation.
  - If the mount seems overdeveloped, then it tends to be aggressive.
  - If it is positioned at the bottom, it indicates a shy and indecisive character; therefore, the person has little chance of gaining success as he lacks the courage to seize the opportunities even if they present themselves.

- **Outer Mount of Mars**

Located between the mount of Mercury and that of the Moon, it represents fortitude, tenacity and the ability to resist pressure. It is also called Mars Major/Superior or Mars Negative and mainly represents self-control and endurance.

- The person with a strong Outer Mars on your hand is steadfast, persevering, and unafraid of danger. Plus, he can handle the humiliations of life. Well-being is generally stable, without ups and downs, as he does not like to risk money.
- If Outer Mars appears overdeveloped, then one lacks courage, usually putting up with what we shouldn't have to put up with.
- If it is flat or set too low, it indicates that a fiery but low stamina individual is unable to remain calm and solve problems tactfully.

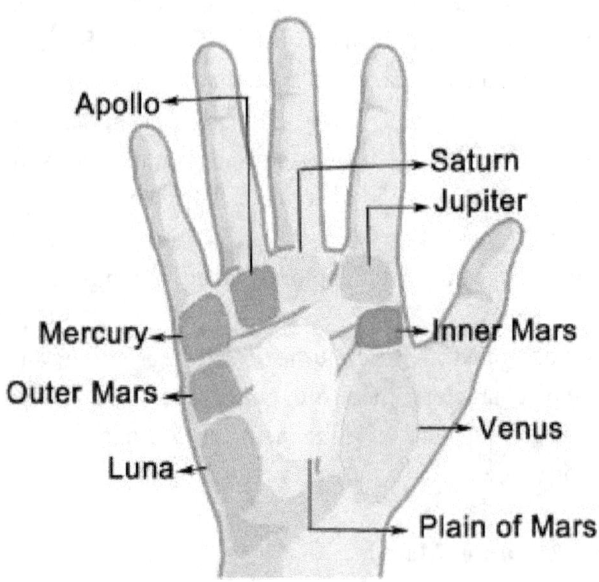



- **The Plain of Mars**

It is the flat area in the center of the hand indicatively between the lines of the heart and the head.

If this area is particularly flat and the various mountains are not very high, starting from the mountains of lower and upper Mars, we are in the presence of a person with little courage in the face of adversity

It is common to observe that the Plain of Mars is hollow, it never gets too protruding.

- If it is wide and flat with no crosses, it is considered a good sign.
- If it's too low and the other Mounts are low too, that's not a good sign. It is possible that one suffers from a lack of vitality and, therefore, it is difficult in life to proceed with one's projects.

**The Lines**

They are the signs that furrow the palm in various directions and represent the most interesting element as, always different from individual to individual, they express the uniqueness and unrepeatability of each of us.

They depict the roads we travel throughout our life with its difficulties and stumbling blocks along the way, with moments of happiness and luck, joys and sorrows.

They are traditionally divided into main ones; line of life, head and heart as present on all hands and secondary: of destiny, happiness and intuition as often absent.

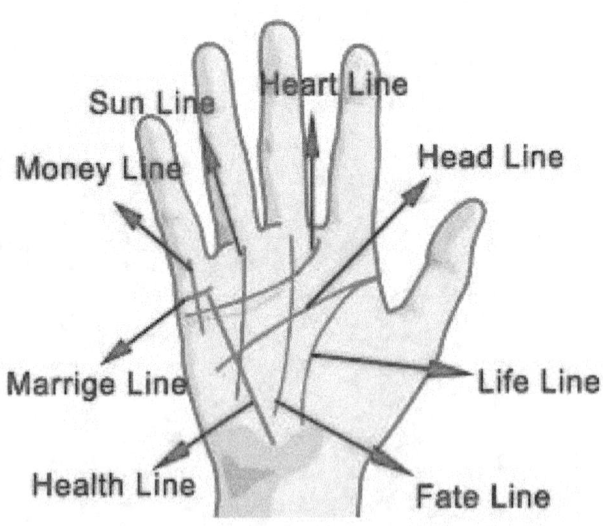

# The Life Line

The Life Line begins at the edge of the hand, between the thumb and forefinger and arcs downward towards the wrist.
It also has the name of Hereditary Line because it gives indications about the state of health and physical constitution.
Contrary to popular belief, its length is not a sure indication of longevity, however, whoever has it well extended and above all marked will generally have a healthy and long life.

- The life line should be read from bottom to top.

The beginning of the line can be located more or less close to the thumb: the closer it is to the thumb, the less importance the individual attaches to ambition and achievement.
A regular shape without signs, more ideal than verifiable, indicates excellent health, balance, vitality, normal sexual appetites, almost a white fly.

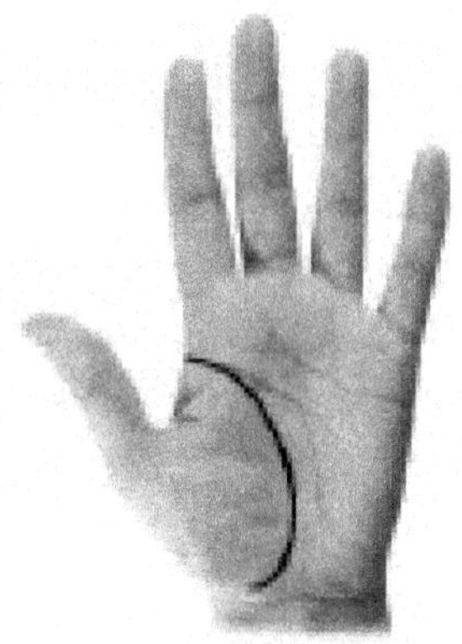

The wider, marked, linear, without smudges it is, the greater the vitality.
If it is narrow and deep, it indicates an introverted and worry-prone temperament.

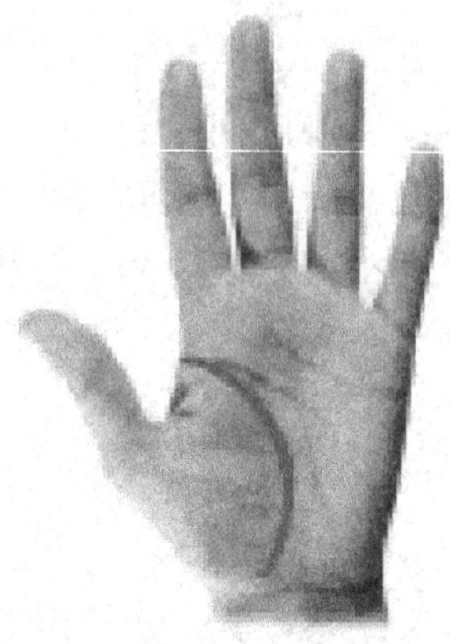

If it is irregular, badly drawn with some uncertain traits, we will be annoyed by continuous small disturbances, nothing serious, it will be enough that in the bad moments, we take things at a more relaxed pace.

If it is short or has a fracture, a shape it has been carrying since birth, then the situation is more complex; according to tradition, categorical in its judgments and tragic in its conclusions, it was a sign of sudden and violent death. Today's conclusions, based on more reliable studies, rule out tragedy even if they acknowledge loss of energy due to accident, illness or, more often, painful separation.

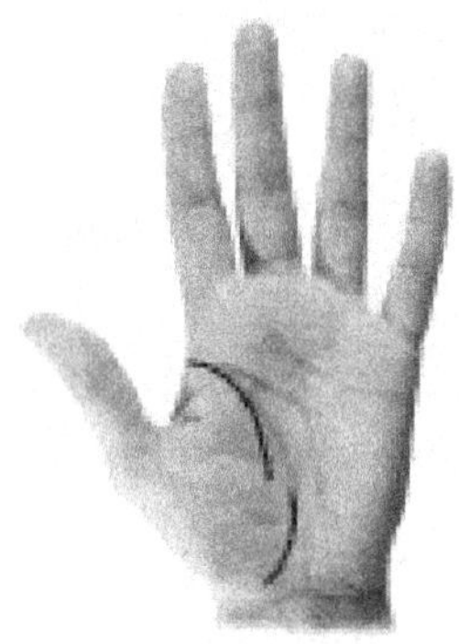

If the final part is divided into many thin stretches like the delta of a river, then the last phase of life will have to be measured with a progressive dispersion of energy which will slow down its normal functions.

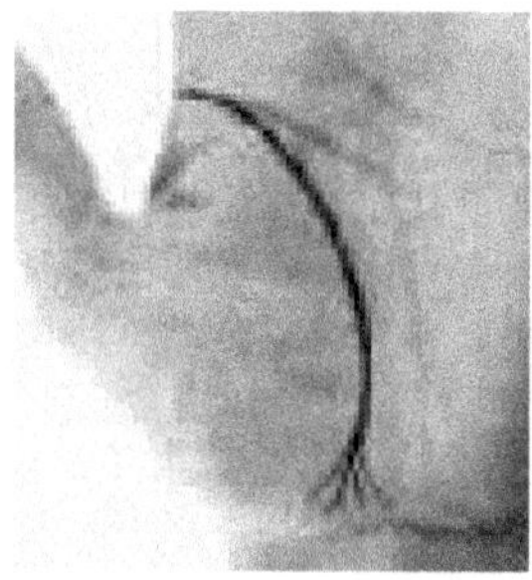

- If the origin of the life line is closer to the base of the index finger (Mount of Jupiter) than to the thumb, Jupiter's influence is greater and conveys ambition and self-confidence.
- If it begins near the birth of the thumb, the influence of Jupiter is reduced and there is an increase in lack of self-confidence coupled with an excessive love of solitude.
- When there is equidistance between the base of the index finger and the birth of the thumb this expresses balance in the personality.

59

- When the line repeats itself and is, therefore, double or branched, it is an indication of sexual potency and vitality.
- Finally, the poorly marked and at the same time faded outline indicates poor health.
- If the line has a fork, it means that the person will have two possibilities to choose from and one will exclude the other.

If you have a line that runs parallel to that of life inside the mount of Venus, then yes, you have a guardian angel, a particular protection from above who has the task of protecting you from any risk and danger and, in case of illness , helps you react vigorously and recover faster. It is also a powerful shield against malice, envy and the evil eye, feelings that lucky people, and the guardian angel is lucky, easily pull on themselves.
If it is continuous and regular, vigilance is constant; if it is shorter or dotted, your "superior defense" takes a few moments of vacation.
If there isn't a line, never mind, you'll only have to walk with your legs.

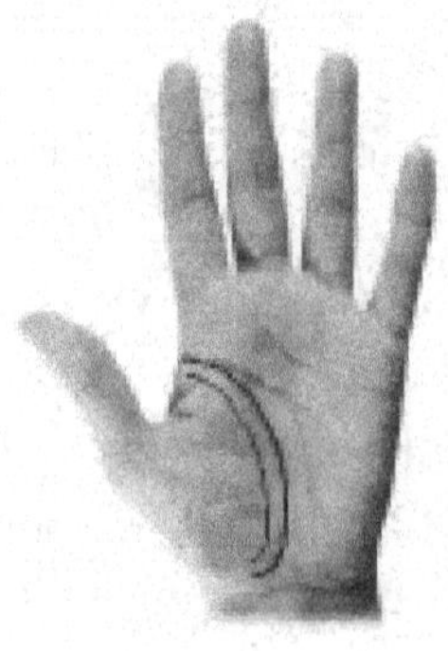

**The Head Line**

This line outlines the signs related to intelligence, attention, memory and mental aptitudes in general.

If the line is curved it is associated with creativity and spontaneity, while if it is straight, the person will have a structured and practical approach to things.

- It therefore suggests whether the individual is prone to creativity and imagination or whether he is a logical and rational person.

It begins under the mount of Jupiter, at the base of the index finger, and winds its way up to the edge of the hand.

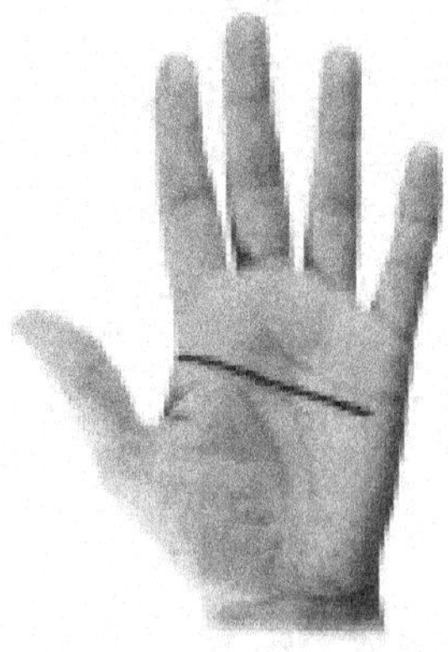

If the line is linked to that of life, we will be dealing with a person who does not have much self-confidence and needs confirmation; if, on the other hand, it is well detached, the subject is very proud and is self-sufficient.

- The best position for this line is where it touches the life line by less than an inch, as it will identify a person capable of calibrating boldness and thoughtfulness.

If it is straight, the imagination is certainly not our forte: we are lucid calculators, skilled speculators capable of making the most of situations to obtain the greatest possible profit.

If the line has a horizontal trend it indicates a propensity for logic, practicality, analytical ability and also a good memory.

When then, in the last stretch, it heads upwards pointing at the base of the little finger, we can safely dedicate ourselves to the professions that handle money, preferably other people's.

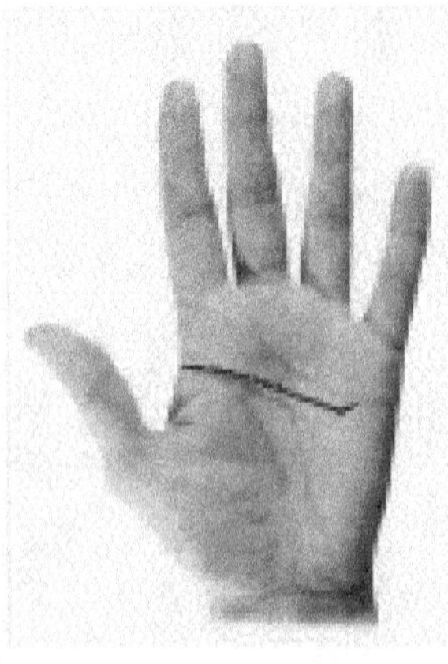

If it curves down, then fantasy and imagination prevail.

When you dive into Monte della Luna let's dedicate ourselves to the study of the past, ancient history, archaeology, any kind of research concerning man's distant roots: an adventurous life à la Indiana Jones can await us.

If too much movement tires us just thinking about it, literature and philosophy are our way; the study of architecture, more concrete and constructive, should also be taken into consideration.

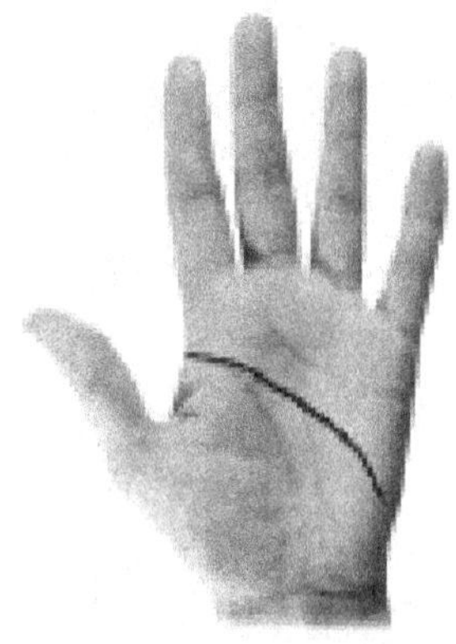

If it curves downwards, but towards the center of the hand in the valley of Neptune, we have the line of the writer or journalist: curiosity towards our surroundings and spirit of observation are the strengths that lead us to the desire and ability to to tell.

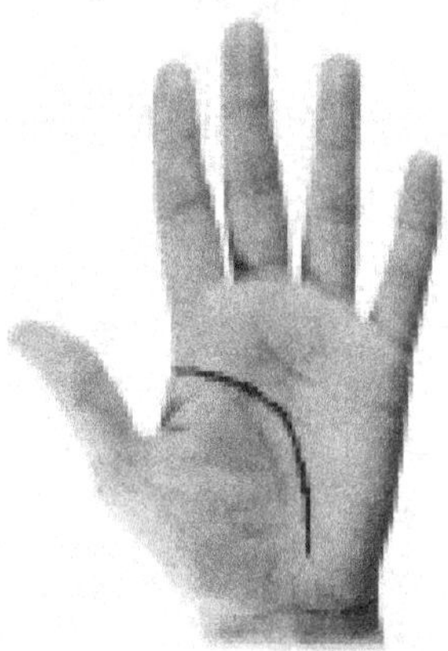

- A short line is an indication of safety, while a long one suggests a great artistic tendency.
- A final fork in addition to creativity also indicates excellent business instincts.

- The wavy line indicates a mind unable to dwell too long on the same subject and prone to distraction.
- A poorly marked and thin line indicates poor ability to concentrate; if, on the other hand, it is too deep, it signals an inclination to perfectionism, with attitudes of meticulousness and quibbling.
- An irregular and discontinuous path denounces a weak will and influenced by the opinions of others, together with a poor memory and a tendency to depression.
- If the head line starts from the waist line at the height of the middle finger, it means that the person is introverted and very attentive; it is also a sign of diligence and dedication at work.
- If the head line starts from the life line, but towards the center of the palm, the person is very thoughtful, often thinks too much and finds it difficult to make decisions.
- If the wisdom line and the life line are separate and distinct from beginning to end, it means that the person is very confident, knows what he wants and knows how to adapt to changes.

**The Heart Line**

The heart line starts between the index and middle fingers and provides indications on emotional capacities and love, but also provides indications on friendship and willingness to altruism; it is the key that helps to understand the quality of the deepest feelings and the way in which each of us relates to others.
The heart line can be read from the little finger to the index finger or vice versa.

- In its tracing it reveals the type of sensitivity, the nature of love, the expectations and the ability to give in every relationship in which emotional exchanges enter.

It can start from under the index finger indicating a very romantic person; under the middle finger, on the other hand, it indicates a dominant and demanding person.

- It is generally believed that the first position is typically female while the second male.

The proximity of this line to the head line is indicative of the subject's ability to balance rationality and emotion; an ideal heart line should appear clear, crisp, with no breaks or lines that intersect it abruptly.
The line of the head and that of the heart form the so-called quadrangle with their paths: when the space between the aforementioned lines is quite large, the subject is generous and tolerant, while if limited, it indicates an introverted and individualistic person.

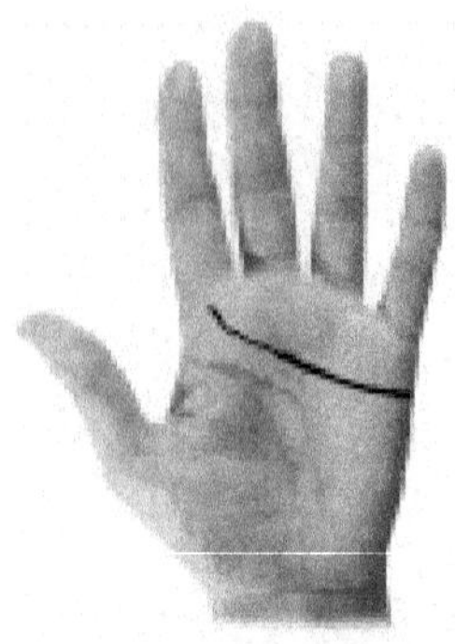

If it ends curving on the mount of Jupiter at the base of the index finger, then we are romantic dreamers, those who present themselves with the flower in hand, those who idealize their love by placing it on a pedestal. Excellent while it lasts, but when we discover that our beloved is just a mere mortal, then love cracks, with each disillusionment the cracks widen and passion inexorably goes out.

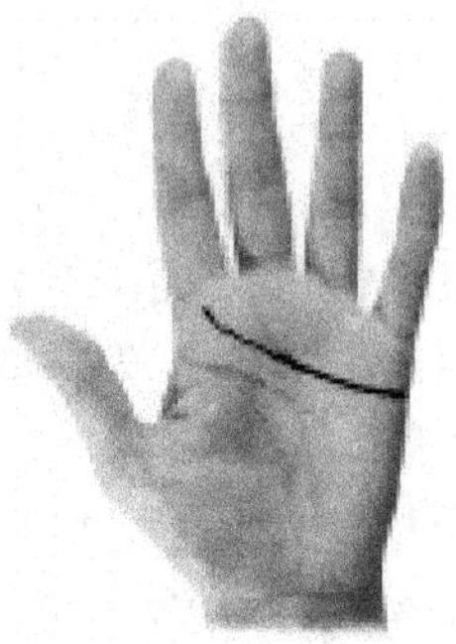

When the line ends at the point where the index and middle fingers meet, the cuddling decreases, not because the affection is less profound, but because it is balanced by a more practical and concrete vision; we are less outgoing and by our nature we prefer to demonstrate feelings through material and tangible facts, rather than with sweet words. This allows us to build, brick by brick, a solid house capable of withstanding all bad weather.

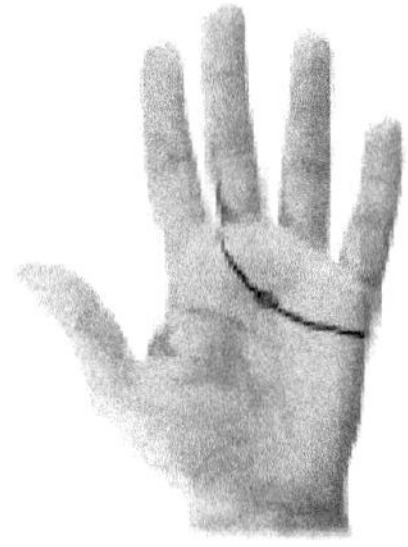

When the line curves abruptly and closes in the middle of the mount of Saturn at the base of the middle finger, then the search for emotions takes place more in the satisfaction of the senses than in the communion of feelings. Our satisfaction is linked more to fleeting relationships that do not create binding bonds and do not require responsibility towards the partner; the problem lies with the other, that if she wants to maintain the often tiring relationship, she must assume the role of maternal and tolerant guide.

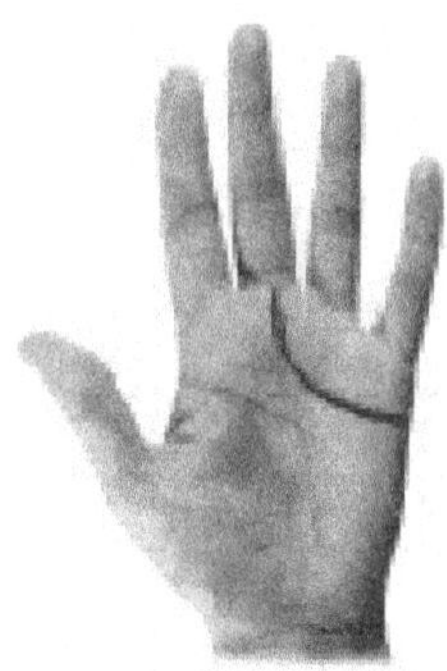

When the line ends by dividing into three branches, which give it the appearance of a trident, then love is luck and success because it brings together the different positive characteristics expressed by the other lines, blends feeling and reason, sensitivity and practical sense and allows the its owner to harmonize with any other types whose true needs it can perceive.

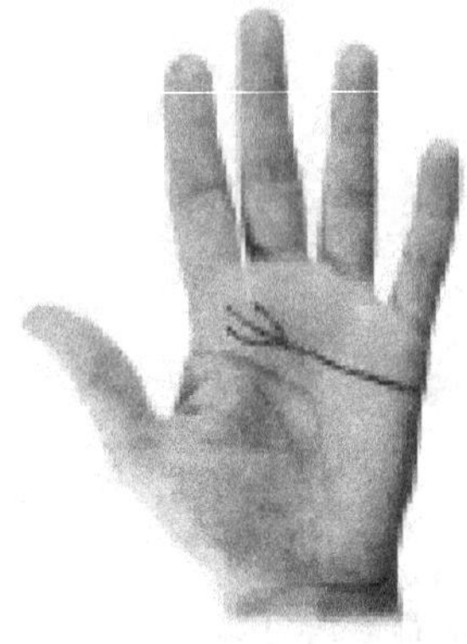

When the line is straight and crosses the entire palm from one side to the other, then love becomes a sense of responsibility and protection, it is the open umbrella that shelters those to whom our affection goes from risks and dangers.

True happiness lies in this mission that fate has entrusted to us and which extends to friends, the group and so on, for which we feel responsible to the point of sacrificing our closest and most intimate family life.

Protection, but also a sense of ownership, and when someone tries to escape our sometimes too suffocating embrace, then jealousies and jolts of pride are unleashed which are quickly overcome because the tasks we feel we have to carry out are more important.

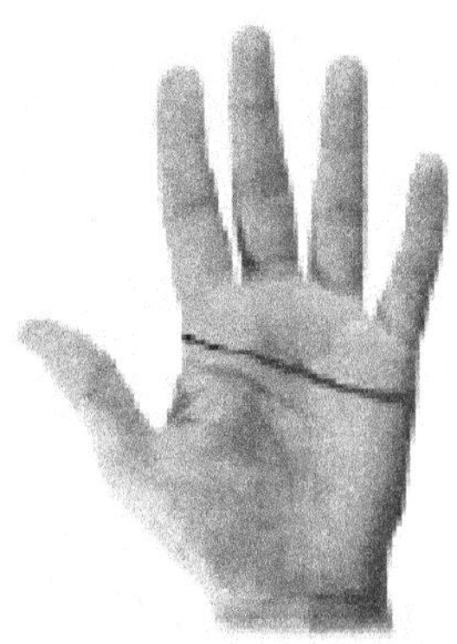

- A regular and well-drawn line indicates generosity, goodness of mind, sensitivity and, therefore, a marked propensity for interpersonal relationships, as well as a certain ease in being satisfied with reaching out in sentimental relationships.
- On the contrary, an irregular line reveals discontinuous loves and lack of emotional balance; if it is instead broken, it can be an indication of infidelity in love.
- The presence of a very long heart line, which crosses the hand horizontally, denounces aridity of soul and irascibility; if it is even longer and surpasses the cut of the hand, it indicates a very passionate temperament, an easy prey to jealousy.
- A short line instead signals the presence of a rational and calculating mind and not inclined to love passions.
- Finally, if it is straight, it reveals coldness and little openness towards feeling, if it is very curved it can show excesses of sensitivity and sentimentality.
- If the love line and the life line meet, it means that the person often feels hurt and does not have good emotional control.

**The letter "M"**

Looking at the folds of our hand we can check if they form the letter "M"; in this case, according to palmistry, we could be a special person.

- The heart line, the head line and the life lines can give rise to this combination.

Anyone who is characterized by this somatic trait has great intuition, as well as great perspicacity and above all brilliant intelligence. Anyone who has the letter "M" on their hand has a gift: understanding if the person in front of them is lying. Furthermore, the person who possesses this characteristic does not lie much and hates being teased. He also has great resourcefulness and is a tough nut to crack.

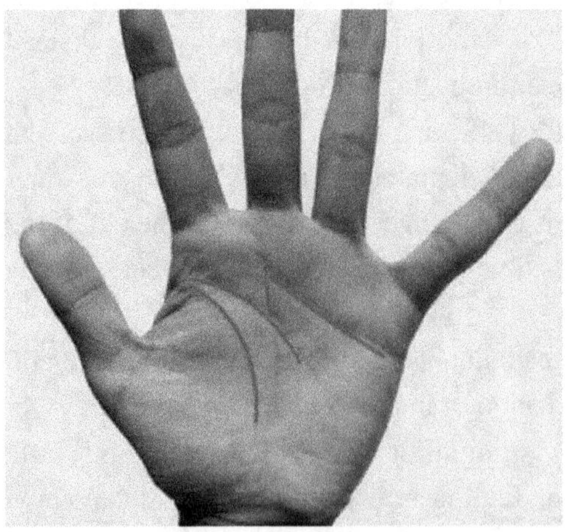

This trait is more pronounced in women than in men, but it is a trait that strongly characterizes both.

Whoever has this characteristic is very sincere and in the same way demands sincerity, moreover, he is endowed with great initiative and is very stubborn and extremely determined.

For this reason, these people are excellent partners both at work and in the relational field; however, they are not easily duped and deceived due to their special gifts.

They never miss an opportunity to improve in their lives and love to challenge themselves constantly.

All those who have the "M" on the palm of their hand are excellent leaders and enjoy good luck due to their particular inclination.

- However, all these characteristics are very rare and not very widespread, if you or someone close to you has them, they must consider themselves very lucky and special.

The meaning is identical both for those who have this letter on one hand and for those who have it on both hands; of course, in case of only one hand with this symbol, the meaning of the other symbol will have to be seen in palmistry: both will act in synergy.

## The Destiny Line

The Destiny Line begins above the wrist and extends vertically to the base of the middle finger; among the secondary ones it is the most important, it is no coincidence that it is also called "Linea della Fortuna", and in the ideal form it is born close to the wrist reaching without interruptions the base of the middle finger.
It is the path that leads to success, without obstacles and with certain results: it expresses the ability of a path that adapts to situations, that knows how to seize the right moments, that lives in harmony with the external environment.
It can take on different paths and different lengths, often appearing fragmented with lines that overlap each other.

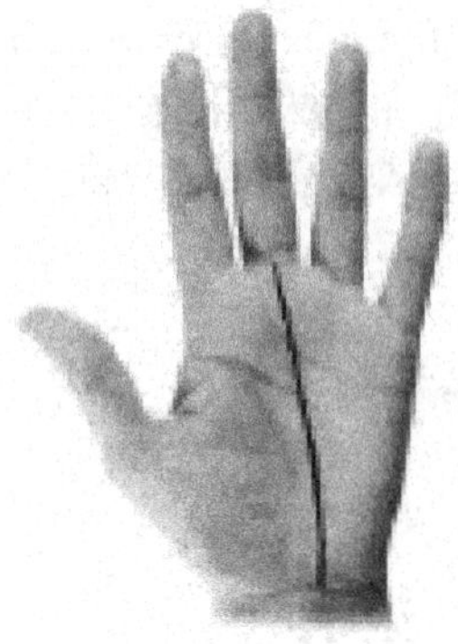

This line notoriously represents the career and the degree of success achieved in one's professional life, as well as the individual aptitude for taking on responsibilities and dealing effectively with demanding situations.
Considering that its presence is not detectable in all hands, its lack may indicate a life without particular professional

significance; therefore, if it isn't there, patience, success is not excluded, but we will have to rely only on our own strength.

The presence, which cannot be excluded, of two distinct and parallel lines of destiny, indicates the duplicity of interests that involves the subject: his personality will constantly require him to cultivate his two passions and aptitudes, which however practical act is always difficult.

When it comes from the mount of Venus, our strength is enterprise, vitality and enthusiasm.

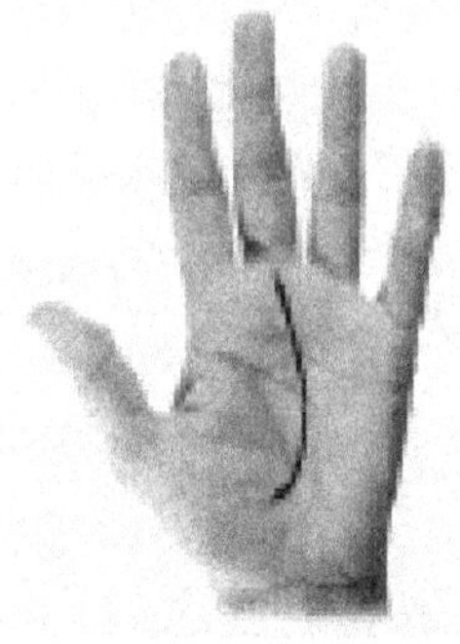

If it comes from the Monte della Luna we are full of imagination, flair and creativity.

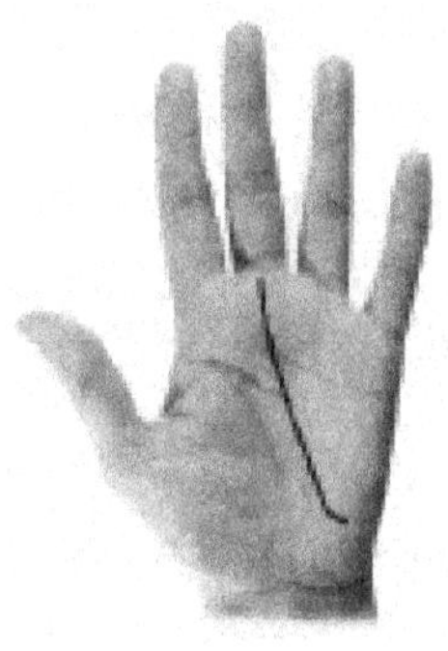

Sections parallel to the main line indicate particularly favorable moments: we can also run some risks because the chances of success are high.

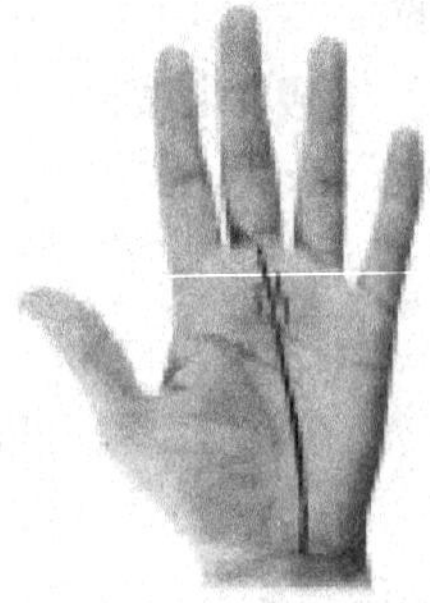

A fragmented line, but regular in its length, gives the eclectic spirit of those who have a thousand interests to experiment with: let's get ready for a dynamic life full of changes.

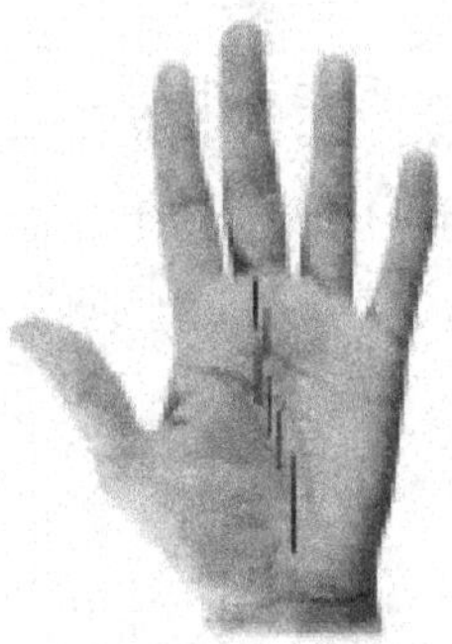

- If the line is thin, you will have a particular predisposition to absorb situations dictated by fate.
- The lesser or greater intensity of the line is proportional to the subject's potential for free will and the ability to take initiative in the entrepreneurial field.

- The possible overlapping of the various traits that compose it suggest that the person tends to get bored immediately and, consequently, always seeks new stimuli and interests.
- When this line joins with the one coming from the mount of the Moon, it shows that the person is inclined to pursue a career in show business as he has a good relationship with the public and with people in general.

**The Line of Happiness**

It originates in the lower part of the palm and winds upwards until it reaches the mount of Apollo at the base of the ring finger.

The Happiness line represents the harmony and optimism achieved with oneself and expresses the ability to enjoy the satisfactions that life can offer.

If it is straight , extended and without interruptions, it indicates the presence of optimism, radiance and sympathy, highlighting great loves (past and/or future) and satisfaction both in the spiritual and material fields of life.

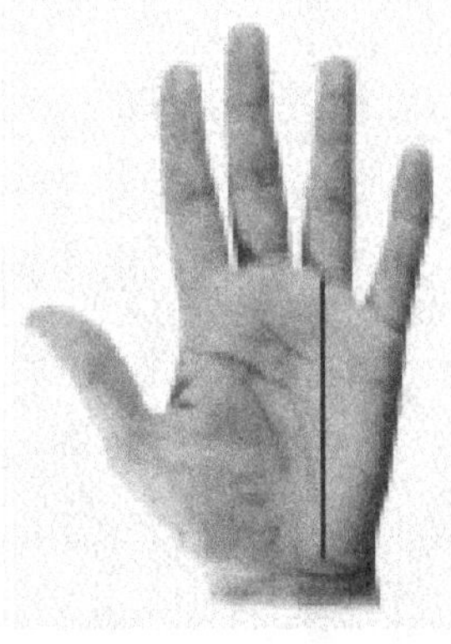

If it is made up of numerous side by side and parallel traits , then we are in the presence of versatile people, endowed with even diversified talents, even if not necessarily developed on a professional level.

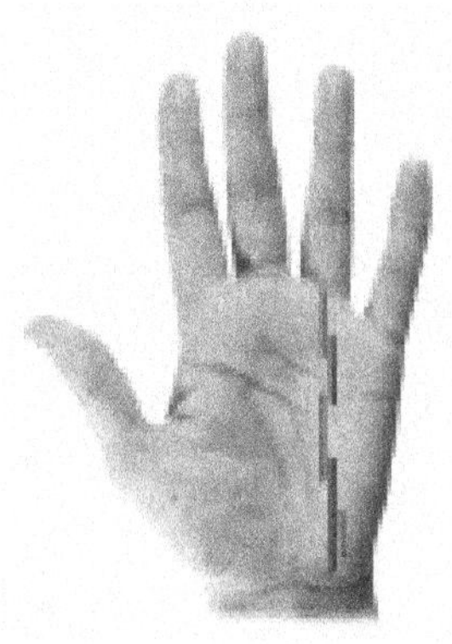

If it appears dotted , then happiness will not be a constant in our life which will see alternating moments of joy and vitality, together with moments of distrust and pessimism.

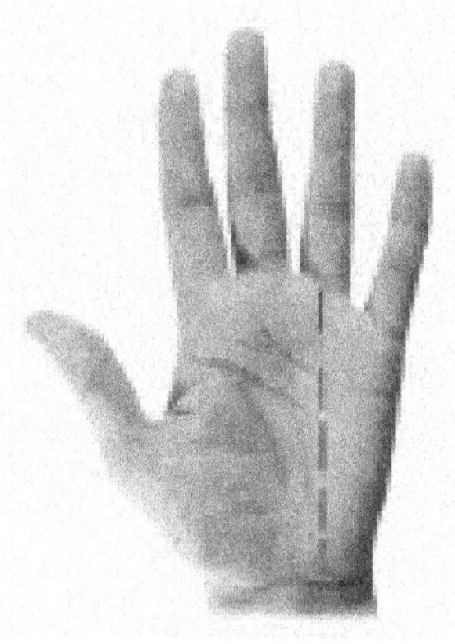

If it is highlighted only in the last stretch on the mountain of Apollo, beyond the heart line, then the satisfaction of what we have built is a goal that we will reach later and with greater effort, but its intensity will be sufficient to repay us for our efforts.

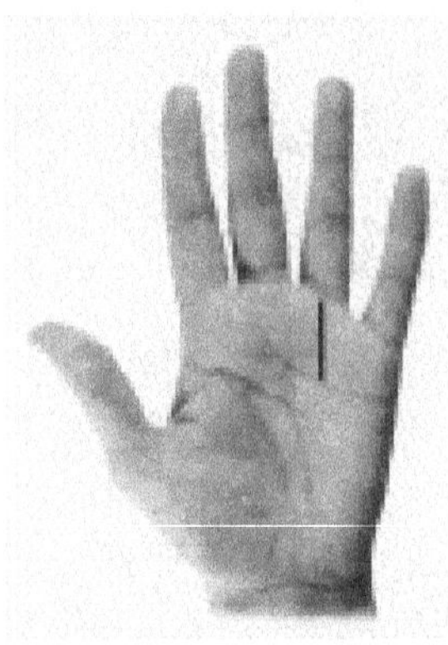

Its presence may not reveal itself in some hands: in this case it does not necessarily mean poverty of talents or a destiny poor in successes, in fact, these can, however, arrive without however involving the satisfaction and degree of happiness attainable in other subjects.

**The Line of Intuition**

The intuition line begins at the bottom of the palm and ends at the base of the little finger.
It expresses a form of sensitivity that allows you to receive vibrations arriving from the outside and to capture sensations otherwise imperceptible to others.

If the line is born near the mount of Venus , intuition turns out to be a natural impulse linked to our most earthly and animal aspect.

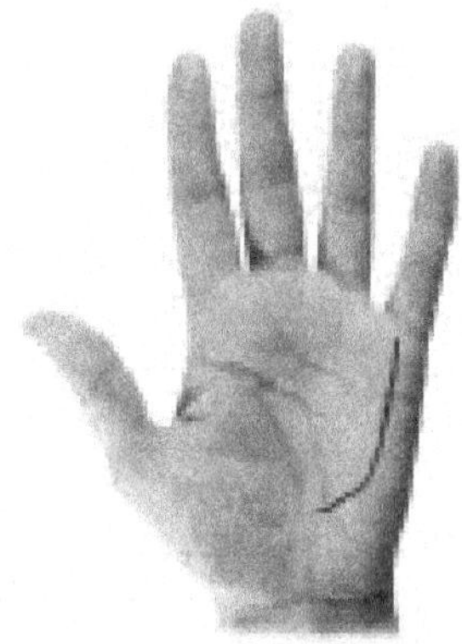

If it is born near the mount of the Moon , intuition acquires a more abstract character, linked to the imagination and to the faculties of foresight.

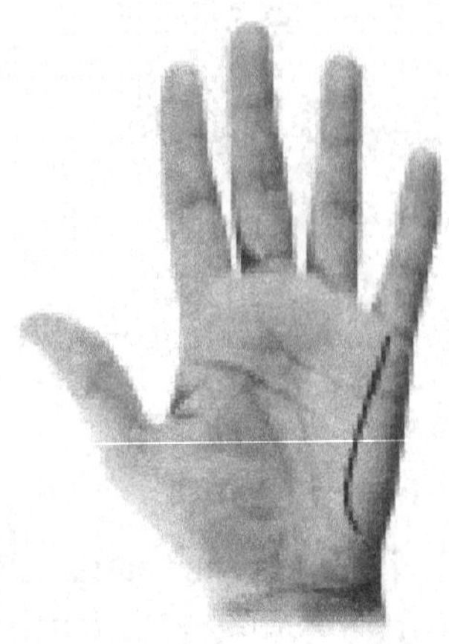

the presence of the line indicates predisposition in business and in all professional fields in which intuition is fundamental, because it allows us to make adequate decisions relying not only on logic but also on irrational perceptions.

If this line is incomplete or poorly drawn, it may indicate an impoverishment of this ability.

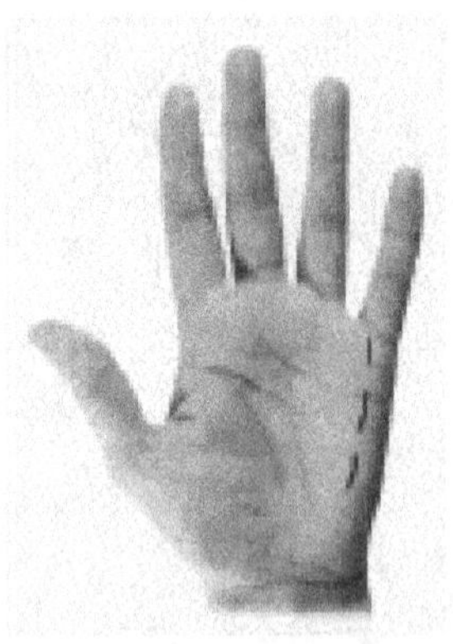

**The Simian Line**

When the lines of the heart and the head coincide or tend to coincide, the line is called simiana.
The term comes from the Latin sīmĭa (monkey), because in some monkeys only one line has been found in the palm.
The presence of the simian line is associated with numerous genetic syndromes: it appears in those with Down syndrome (50% of cases), Patau syndrome (60%), Edward syndrome (30%) and cat (90%).

- Healthy individuals with simian line are a minimal percentage of the world population, about 1-2%.

Science has not yet managed to establish whether in these cases the presence of the simian line is to be considered a mere accident or not; the simian line occurs in one in thirty people and is much more common in men than in women.

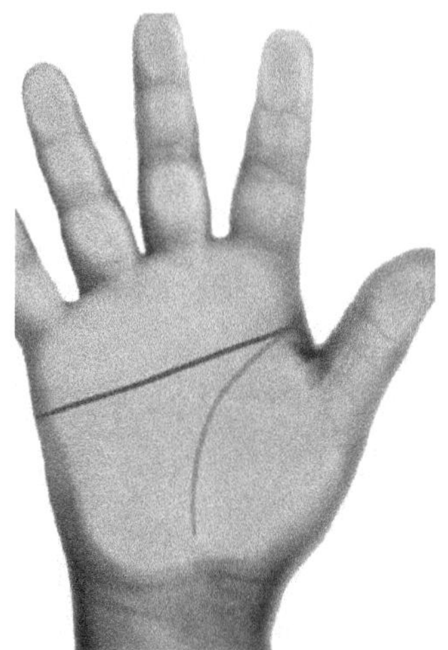

Almost all palmists agree in affirming a very simple thing: those with the simian line cannot keep rationality and emotion separate; this characteristic can lead to living anything in a particularly passionate and intense way, but it can also lead to fanaticism and madness.

- It is identified as a very lucky sign that denotes great capacity for mental concentration, power of imagination and according to tradition it can sometimes also lead to clairvoyance.

The line can be held in both hands, but also in only one of the two.
There are several famous people who have at least one simian line: Thom Yorke, Armin van Buuren, Tony Blair, Hillary Clinton, Robert De Niro, Buddha, Nick Rhodes, Rasputin, Rainn Wilson.

**Winner announced**

It is the line that announces a winning game, one of the consistent ones that suddenly distorts existence, dyeing the future pink.

Very long and thin, it arises from the mount of Venus and, crossing the palm in all its width, enters that of Mercury at the base of the little finger.

- It must be regular, without interruptions or signs that hinder its path: for these reasons, and because it can appear and disappear in a few days, it is better to look for it with a magnifying glass before building ruinous castles in the air.

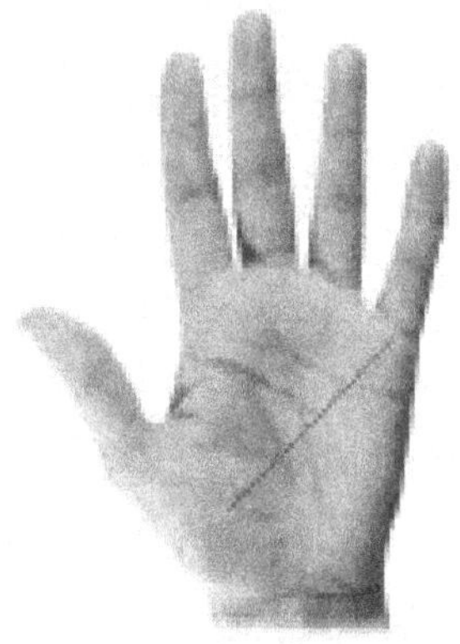

**The Line of Excess**

It is the line that unites the heart and the head in a single stroke, blending emotions and reason together.

Then you are a person in perpetual intimate conflict, with an excessive and impetuous temper in all your manifestations.

When you love, all energy turns to love, therefore, total devotion and passion; when you dedicate yourself to something else you have an excellent capacity for isolation and concentration that can reach clairvoyance.

It's a pity that those who frequent you encounter some difficulty in understanding your sudden changes of mood and in following you in your acrobatic leaps from one pole to another.

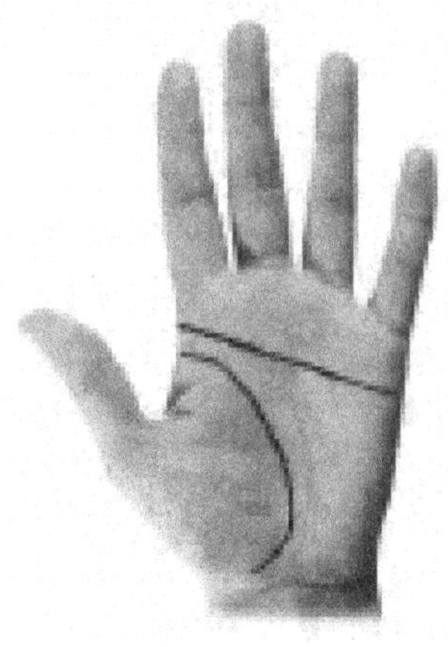

## Hot Line

It is a short horizontal line, defined via lasciva, which unites, in the lower part of the hand near the wrist, the mount of Venus with that of the Moon, decisively entering the latter.
It takes different shapes and can appear as a straight, curved or wavy horizontal stroke.

- The name was decided by the ancient fortune tellers who had found libertine behaviors in those who owned this line.

The meaning that we tend to give today does not differ much from the old interpretation, indeed, it even broadens the concept: its presence, in fact, signals the search for strong and transgressive emotions in the specifically sentimental and erotic field as the ancients intended, but to this is added the need for intense sensations in the various interests that life offers and to enhance them he does not disdain the help of alcohol and drugs.

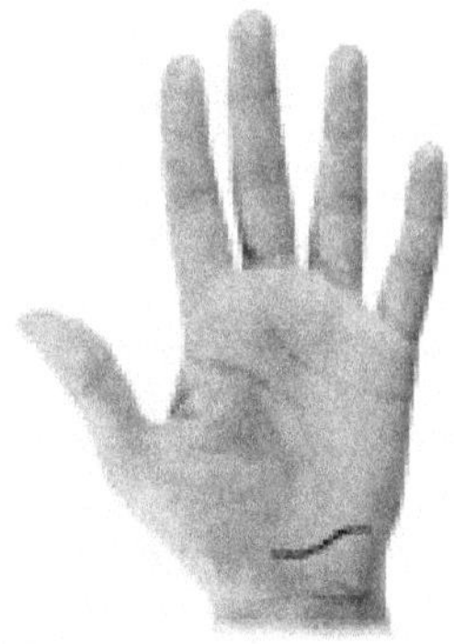

## The Marriage Line

The marriage line starts approximately above the beginning of the heart line.
A person will likely have more than one line; maybe even four or five, but that doesn't necessarily mean that there will be as many weddings. Rather, they indicate the relationships that deeply mark the individual. It will be the sentimental experiences, sweet or bitter, that will be remembered for a lifetime.

Each line will indicate, based on depth and length, how deep the mark left by the person you met was.
A very approximate time scale can be deduced by observing whether the line in question is close to the heart line (youth) or close to the finger joint (old age).

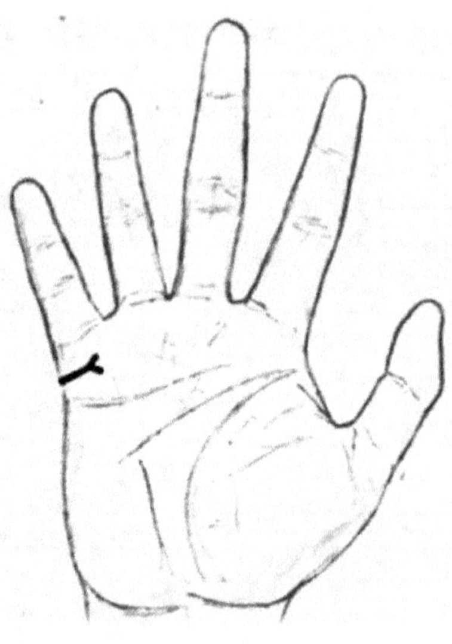

- If there is a bifurcation at the end of the marriage line, this indicates that the contrasts of opinion in the couple are prevailing and this leads to separation or divorce. The length of the two branches of the bifurcation influence the intensity of the contrast between the spouses: the greater the length, the greater the contrast.

- If there is a vertical dash that cuts the marriage line this will be affected by emotional and economic difficulties that will hinder married life which could end if the spouses are unable to deal with the difficulties together.

- If two parallel lines are close to each other and of the same length this indicates two important relationships at the same time, conflicting with each other, up to the exclusion of one in favor of the other, with a divorce and a remarriage. The two lines must be observed carefully: to have the same importance they must be of the same color and depth; in fact, if one of the two is not deep or well colored, it represents a relationship of affection or a non-loving feeling.

- An island on the marriage line indicates arguments and quarrels that can lead to marital separation; the position of the island on the line indicates the period of difficulty: if it is at the beginning of the line, the problems will arise at the beginning of the marriage, if it is at the end, they will occur at the end of married life.

- A line of influence ascends from Mount of the Moon and crosses the line of Destiny. If a line of influence originating in the Mount of the Moon ascends and meets the Destiny line, this is a good omen and indicates that the marriage will be happy and successful. However, if the line of influence crosses and cuts the line of Destiny, this indicates that the relationship will soon end or there will be an estrangement and a pause for reflection on whether to continue the loving relationship.

## The Line of the Sun

The Sun line is a hand line that is short and parallel to the Destiny line and mainly shows us the ability, talent and popularity that can lead to success.
Hence, it is also called the success line.

- In general, a long Sun line is better than a short one, and people with a Sun line are more talented; moreover, it is considered a sister line of the Destiny line which could support and enhance it, as a vertical line of expression.

The Sun line or Apollo line is one of the secondary lines in palm reading; it is so called because it originates from the Mount of the Moon (located on the base of the palm, little finger side) and rises upwards to the Mount of the Sun (located under the ring finger which is also called Apollo's finger).

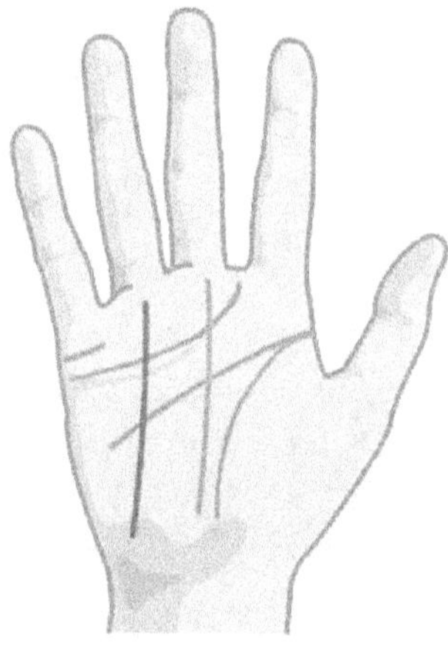

If it starts from the base of the palm and goes straight to the top, it is thought to be auspicious; indicates good luck for wealth and marriage.

If it starts at the base of the palm and ends at the center of the hand, it shows great success in young age and decline from middle age. This could be caused by satisfaction with the current state, which , therefore, makes one stop making great efforts in life from middle age.

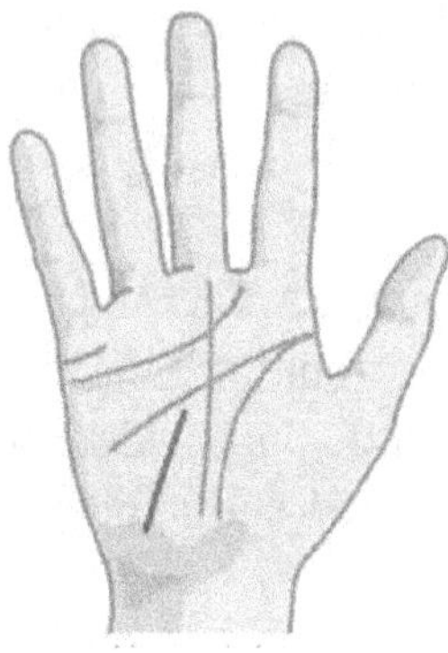

If the sun line starts at the Mount of Venus (the portion of the palm surrounded by the lifeline at the base of the thumb) and extends to the base of the ring finger, it indicates the possibility of gain, wealth, and fame with the help of family.

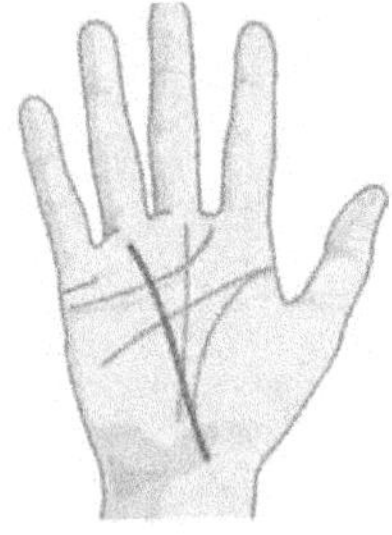

If the sun line starts from the Upper Mount of Mars (located between the head line and the heart line, under the little finger)

and ends at the base of the ring finger, it indicates a successful career.

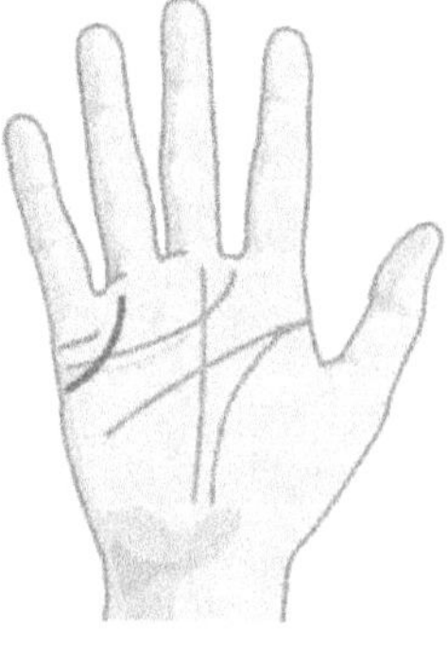

If the sun line starts from the Destiny line and extends upwards, it indicates outstanding achievement and respect from others due to our great effort and hard work.

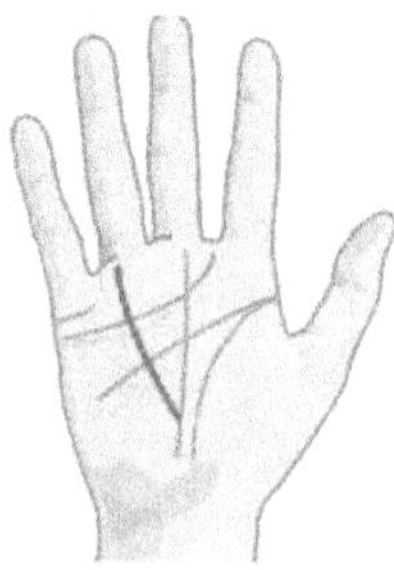

If the line starts at the Mount of the Moon (located at the base of the palm, little finger side) and extends upwards, it shows that one can achieve success with the help and support of others. This type of line can mainly be owned by musicians, writers and entertainers.

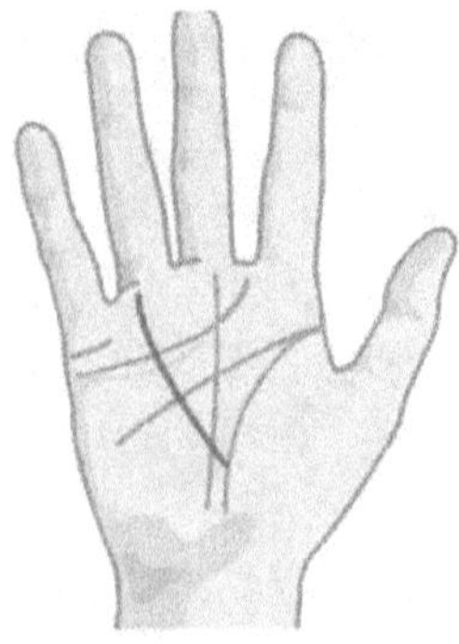

In the end:

- If the Destiny line is there but the Sun line is short, try as hard as you can, it will be difficult to gain recognition and success.
- Conversely, even if the Destiny line is not long or linear, but if one has a strong Sun line, one is able to get help and recognition, and thus achieve success.

**The Health Line**

It is also called Mercury Line or Inner Dialogue Line; in many people it does not appear, but when it is present, it arises from the base of the hand and travels upwards, towards the Mount of Mercury, under the little finger.
The Health line in palm reading is associated with a person's health condition.
There is no fixed location of its starting point: it can start at the base of the little finger and extend along the palm to the base of the thumb, or, it can start below the heart line and finish at the life line without joining it.
In Chinese palmistry, the Health line is also called the Unhealthy Line, because it usually appears in the hands of the person who is not healthy enough.
This does not mean that all types of health lines are bad. A straight line that does not touch the Life line usually indicates good health.
If the health line is absent, that's a good sign; it means that you are healthy and have no health problems.

- A wavy line indicates potential health problems in the digestive system and a decline in liver or gallbladder function; there is a high probability of suffering from gastrointestinal disorders. If it is bent into a large arc, it shows a great loss of strength or stamina.

- A broken line shows that digestive system function is declining; if the broken lines are terraced, the situation is worse.

- If the Health line is crossed by a few short lines, it indicates bad health and one tends to be prone to accidents.

- If the Health line is very short or consists of many short lines, it is also an indication of ill health.

- If it crosses the Head line, in general, those with a long Health line are usually intellectuals. But if the Health line crosses the Head line, it shows that health can be affected by excessive mental fatigue. Particularly after middle age, one can find himself in a state of health that requires more rest and care.

- If it extends to the mons de venus which is at the base of the thumb, there is weakness in the circulatory system. Care should be taken for heart disease or a brain hemorrhage. It is possible to imagine the period by calculating the point of intersection of the two lines.

- If it touches the Life line and ends there, it is an ominous sign for health. You may have a weak cardiovascular system which negatively affects normal blood circulation.

- If it starts from the Heart Line and ends at the Head Line, it suggests that the nervous system is the weak link in case of accidents.

- If two lines of Health cross each other it is an indication of lack of vital energy, weak health and long-term chronic diseases that are not easy to cure.

**The particular signs**

Often on the hands, with careful observation and perhaps with the help of a magnifying glass, you notice signs, small alterations present on mountains and lines that sometimes appear and disappear within a few days, sometimes remain as indelible signs that denounce or announce moods, intimate and external manifestations, messages of destiny.

- Identifying and interpreting them means preparing to face, in the best possible condition, what awaits us, both in the beautiful where waiting for the happy event is easy in itself, but knowing it first helps not to waste it, and, above all, in the ugly, where often the mere knowledge of a difficult moment actively contributes to overcoming it.

Even in the heaviest situations, which we will inevitably have to face, awareness sets in motion defense mechanisms and activates, often unconsciously, the will and the deepest reserves that allow us to overcome difficulties and obstacles.

**Cross**

It is formed by two short crossed strokes and is almost always an indication of tribulations, troubles, with only one positive position.

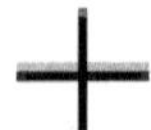

If we find it:
- On the mount of Jupiter, at the base of the index finger, everything is fine, it warns us that an important love encounter is approaching, the classic love at first sight: let's sharpen our antennae and look around before it runs away.
- On the mount of Venus, we sharpen our weapons, a sentimental "storm" approaches, quarrels with thunder and lightning.
- On the mount of Saturn, at the base of the middle finger, let's get ready to support a period of pessimism and loneliness. Justified by external factors or by intimate sensations, a dark cloak will descend upon us, formed by apprehension, a sense of tragedy and anguish, which will be our company until the cross disappears.
- On the mount of Mercury, at the base of the little finger, beware of money and risky speculation, they could cost us dearly.

**Star**

It is made up of numerous sections that radiate from a central point and has the appearance of an asterisk. It is always auspicious and heralds sudden success.

If it shines:

- On the mount of Venus, heralds a period of rewarding love life in which sex, love and passion will play an important role.

- On the mount of Jupiter, it announces success and fame in the field of work.

- On the mount of Apollo, at the base of the ring finger, happiness is more intimate than those that arrive suddenly and without explanation, but which fill the heart with joie de vivre.

- On the mount of Mercury, success is financial, it announces the good harvest that follows brilliant and acute intuitions.

**Island**

It has the shape of a bean and appears on the lines which, for a more or less short stretch, split in two and then close again.

If it appears:

- On the lifeline it's about health: we will face a period of physical instability that will slow down every initiative.

- On the head line, better to postpone the preparation of important choices, the ability to concentrate and the quality of psychic tension are not the best.

- On the line of the heart, it announces a period of sentimental difficulty, certainly not a catastrophe, but a phase tormented by misunderstandings and detachment.

If there is more than one, then the search for a soul mate will be long and moments of great tenderness and participation will alternate with moments of disappointment and detachment.

## Square

It is a drawing made up of four lines with the appearance of a square or a rhombus. It expresses different meanings depending on where it occurs.

If it appears:

- On the line of life, usually straddling a fracture in the line itself, it indicates protection from the threat that the fracture entails. It often forms a few months before the date of danger, and disappears some time later, once its function has finished.

- On the mount of Jupiter, he reveals a natural aptitude for passing on his knowledge to others. It is, in fact, known as the teacher's square.

- On the mount of Saturn, it represents a shield against personal adversities which usually cause pessimism and depression. It encloses in healthy isolation.

**Triangle**

It is a drawing made up of three lines with the appearance of a triangle of different conformations. It means success and wisdom.

If it appears:

- On the mount of Jupiter, he reveals his natural talent for directing and good organizational skills. It announces commitments, but also satisfactions.

- On the mount of Saturn, it expresses the predisposition to occultism and the mystical tendency. It requires moments of isolation and detachment from everyday reality.

- On the mount of Mercury, it indicates business acumen. It allows for steps that may appear rash and risky to others.

- On the Mount of the Moon, it indicates the possession of paranormal abilities. If then, the mount itself is of a more intense pink color than the rest of the hand, then we are also endowed with clairvoyance.

## Grill

It has the shape of a net and appears on some mountains signaling a momentary drop in energy.

If it appears:

- On the mount of Venus, it communicates that it is time to momentarily pull the oars in the boat or, at the very least, slow down our general rhythms. He advises us to take everything more calmly.

- On the mount of Jupiter, it expresses the anxious fear of a choice of which we are not certain, a task which we are unable to complete and which is tiring us out. It is better to set aside and postpone until the mind is calmer.

- On the Mount of Apollo, it warns that our creativity is going through a period of fog and confusion. Better to let your imagination rest and devote yourself to more concrete tasks.

- On the mount of Mercury, it indicates that we are conducting business in a disorganized way and without a precise aim. It would be advisable to wait for the grid to begin to fade.

**Bar**

It is a small stretch that crosses the lines and represents an obstacle of low intensity and short duration.

It acquires different meanings according to the lines it crosses. If it crosses:

- The life line represents a passing malaise.

- The line of the head signals a moment of anxiety.

- The line of the heart reveals a sentimental disagreement.

- The line of fate indicates a career hitch.

- The line of happiness announces a fleeting cloud.

**Fingers**

Depending on their size, fingers have various meanings.

- Long fingers indicate a careful, patient, meticulous and methodical person; if, however, they are excessively long, they indicate that the person is excessively meticulous, and are also a sign of vanity.
- Short fingers indicate capacity for synthesis and ready intuition, as well as physical and thought dynamism.
- Medium length fingers indicate balance between intelligence and instinct, ability to analyze and synthesis together; those fingers in which the index has the same length as the palm are of medium length.
- Very thick fingers denote materiality but also the possibility of practical success, while thin fingers indicate an idealistic person; if they are in an unharmonious hand, they indicate cunning and deceit.
- Fat fingers denote a tendency towards material things, well-being, the pleasures of the flesh and the table, while thin fingers characterize cerebral individuals, alien to material pleasures and tense in the success of their aspirations.
- If the fingers end in the shape of a spatula, they always announce brusque manners, especially if the life line is deep and red, but if the heart line is accentuated it also means a good heart.
- Conical toes, i.e. those that taper at the tip, indicate good receptivity.
- The square toes, i.e. those that have the last phalanx of an equal size from the base to the tip, represent balance, reflection, order.

- Well-proportioned toes announce a good disposition.

In general , the indications that can be drawn of a psychological nature from the measurement of the fingertips are the following:

- First phalanx, at the tip of the finger: if more developed than the others, it indicates greater impressionability.
- Second phalanx, intermediate: if more developed it indicates a reasoning and scholarly character as well as spirituality.
- Third phalanx, close to the palm: if longer and thicker it denotes a calm and indolent character.

If the three phalanges of the four fingers are of the same length and thickness, it is a sign that the subject is a balanced and just person.

Smooth fingers reveal tact, inspiration, spontaneity, first impulse; if particularly smooth they indicate lightheadedness, caprice and lightness. If the smooth fingers are square, there will be greater balance between inspiration and reason; the subject will love the arts, literature, will have positive ideas.
The smooth spatula fingers indicate a compromise between order and the appearance of order: you will have a materialistic sensibility that makes you appreciate the utilitarian aspect of things and activities rather than delicacy as well as positive intelligence.
In knotted fingers, two types of knots are distinguished.
Between the first phalanx (the one that has the nail) and the second phalanx is the philosophical knot; the knot placed between the second and third phalanx is the knot of the material order.

Knotless fingers belong to the hands of artists: in fact, even if they give themselves a positive purpose, artists always proceed more by inspiration than by reasoning; more for fantasy and feeling than for adherence to the reality of life.

Knots change the characteristics of the fingers.
The first knot, the one closest to the nail, is called the "philosophical knot"; it is the node of reasoning and discussion and represents the tendency to analysis and order in ideas: the more the node is pronounced, the more these qualities are affirmed.
The second knot, which ties the second phalanx to the one at the base of the fingers, is called the "material knot"; the more pronounced it is, the more it indicates the tendency towards material order which can lead to an excess of meticulousness.

**The Thumb**

The thumb corresponds to the planet Venus.

It is the finger of will and logic; the study of this finger is particularly important.

From the shape of the thumb, the indication of the qualities of the individual's character can be modified, and even completely changed: in fact, this finger represents the will and the most precious gift of the spirit, which is logic.

The development of the thumb is in proportion to the development of the mental faculties: individuals with a dull mind have a weak thumb and often keep it hidden in their fist like newborns, idiots from birth generally have it atrophied or even without it; in fact, they lack will and logic.

If the thumb protrudes backwards it indicates stubbornness and an aggressive nature, if instead it turns towards the other fingers it indicates a nervous and simulating nature.

In this finger we distinguish the root, i.e. the mount of Venus, then the second phalanx and the first phalanx with the nail.

- The very developed root of the thumb, mount of Venus, indicates sensuality which can be dominated if the first phalanx, a sign of will, is long.
- The second phalanx, the logic, if it is longer than the first denotes weak will and more logic and reasoning but indecision: if it is much longer it indicates ease of discouragement and great changeability of mood. If it is equal in length to the first phalanx it means that logic and will are in equal measure and determine balance.

- The first phalanx, the one that carries the nail, represents the will. If it is long and strong, it is a sign of powerful and energetic will and a lot of self-confidence. If the phalanx is very long and thick, the will will reach tyranny: there will be much pride. If the phalanx is of medium length, there will only be passive resistance due to inertia, equal mood, indecision. If the phalanx is very short it indicates an absolute lack of will, indifference, mood changes without important reasons.

The thumb is associated with the 3rd Chakra, Mars, the fire element, the Lung Meridian, vitality, instincts, libido, energy, creative power.

Its energy feeds the energy of the other fingers, absorbs excess energy and restores balance in the hand; to be able to do it fully it is necessary to free oneself from irritation in the face of the difficulties and trials of Life.

On the physical level it manages the throat, neck, brain, pineal and pituitary.

The spontaneous overlapping of one thumb over the other indicates whether we are head or heart types; there is a quick and easy way that allows us to know which side we belong to.

Let's try to cross our fingers spontaneously without thinking about it, as we'll happen to do who knows how many times a day: we'll realize we're always doing the gesture in the same way and if we try the opposite, the position will seem forced and unnatural.

- If it's the right hand above the left, it means that we belong to the group of concrete people, those who "things need to be reasoned about, you need to use your head" and then logic, in the end, will prevail over sentiment; of course, love is as important as for anyone else and passions are sincere, but the last word of law will take its toll.

- If, on the contrary, it is the left thumb that covers the right, then we find ourselves in the other group, the equally numerous but more romantic one, in the company of those who cannot silence emotions in decisive moments, those who "feeling it is the voice of the soul, the heart is not in command" and then, in the final skirmish, the reasons of reason slowly fade away and the heart will beat the last note.

**The Index**

The index corresponds to the planet Jupiter.
It is the finger of religion, of success, of fortune, of ambition, of sensuality.
Generally in all its forms it indicates self-love, ambition and pride.

- Only if it is short does it indicate goodness and a benevolent character towards others.
- If it is particularly long, it is a sign of pride and a tendency to dominate.
- If the finger is pointed it will indicate intuition and love for nature.
- If the finger is square, it denotes a tendency to seek truth in relation to nature.

The index is associated with the 4th Chakra, Jupiter, the air element, the Stomach Meridian and the Large Intestine Meridian, intuition, inspiration, acceptance, welcome, self-esteem and self-affirmation.
Everything is achieved if Man gets rid of Anger and Violence.
Physically it manages the eye, the maxillary and frontal sinuses, the stomach, the pancreas, the large intestine.

**The Middle**

The middle finger corresponds to the planet Saturn.
It is the planet of sadness and melancholy, but the finger has the characteristics of prudence, intelligence, patience.

- If it is pointed, i.e. tapering towards the top, it indicates an accommodating character, lightness and even dryness of heart.
- If it is square, it promises balance and reflection but a tendency to melancholy and pessimism.
- If it is spatula shaped, it denotes activity but a temperament prone to melancholy.
- If the finger is long, it heralds discouragement easily, while if it is short, it indicates that the subject accepts life's circumstances philosophically.

The middle chakra is associated with the 5th Chakra, Saturn, the ether element, the Gall Bladder Meridian and the Circulation Meridian. It is the Door to heaven, purity, ambition, initiative, action, order.
Everything is possible if you cultivate patience and humility.
Physically it manages the eye, the maxillary and frontal sinuses, the gallbladder, circulation, fatigue syndromes.

**The Ring Finger**

The ring finger corresponds to the Sun.
Indicates stability, idealism, artistic skills, critical thinking and success.
It is the finger of Apollo, that is of material and spiritual wealth.

- If it is pointed it means intuition and sensitivity for beauty.
- If square, it announces artistic tendencies and the possibility of creation: reason is applied in art as in life.
- When the ring finger is short it indicates that one has the faculty to perceive but not to create.
- If it is long, it announces a lot of ambition, artistic talent, desire for fame and a willingness to gamble.

The ring finger is associated with the 1st Chakra, Apollo, the sun, the earth element, the Liver Meridian and the Triple Warmer, energy, resistance, serenity, hope, empathy, obtainable when the Man knows how to live in poverty and is responsible for what he thinks, says and does (Karma).
Physically, it manages the ear, the maxillary and frontal sinuses, the liver, the immune and thermoregulation system, and headaches.

**The Little Finger**

The little finger corresponds to the planet Mercury.

It is the finger of medicine, business, study, sociability and cunning. The little finger is associated with the 2nd Chakra, Mercury, the water element, the Heart Meridian, the Small Intestine Meridian, the Meridian of the Kidneys and Bladder, creativity, beauty, clarity, sexuality, communication, emotions.
Everything is achieved when man learns to perform menial tasks and frees himself from criticism and judgment.
Physically it manages the ear, the maxillary and frontal sinuses, the heart, the kidneys, the bladder, abdominal pain, excessive weight.

- The little finger that ends in a point is a sign of intuition and skill; if the top knot is highly developed, it is a sign of aptitude for science and perspicacity: if it is more marked, the second knot indicates business ability.
- If the little finger is twisted, badly made, it belongs to very intelligent people who do not achieve much in life because they are imprudent.
- If the finger is square, it indicates aptitude for study and research based on logic.
- If the finger is shaped like a spatula, it indicates activity, love for active sciences such as mechanics.

**The Phalanxes**

The three phalanges of the fingers represent the three worlds of our existence:

- The first phalanx responds to the divine thing.
- The second in the natural world.
- The third in the material world.

These phalanges are unequal in length and thickness, and according to these proportions and to which finger they belong, they acquire a different meaning.

In ancient times the doctors, with Hippocrates first, also affirmed that the finger of Jupiter was related to the liver; the finger of Saturn, and particularly that of the left hand, sympathized with the spleen, and the ring finger, the finger of Apollo, with the heart.

The phalanx, or third phalanx, or palmar phalanx, connects the finger to the palm of the hand and symbolically represents the "material reality".

- A particularly evident and swollen phalanx indicates sensuality and a propensity for comfort.
- A very long phalanx signals an existence predominantly dominated by material interests.

The falangina, or second phalanx, is located in an intermediate position between the phalanx and the small joint and symbolically represents the "practical sense".

- A particularly long joint indicates the presence of a notable practical sense, while if it is very short it expresses difficulty in dealing with everyday problems.

The phalanx, or first phalanx, or nail phalanx, is the part of the finger
which includes the nail and symbolically represents "ideas".

- A particularly long joint, more frequent in hands with a narrow palm, signals idealism, mysticism and indicates the prevalence of thought over action.
- The joint with a "waterdrop" profile indicates a remarkable tactile sensitivity which makes manual activities of great finesse possible.

## Index: Water finger

- If the first phalanx is relatively long, the divine side will predominate, i.e. intuition and religion.
- If the second is longer, ambition predominates and the positive side will prevail.
- The most developed and longest third phalanx will indicate the proud will to reach the top and dominate.

## Middle, or central, or Cordial: finger of the Earth

- If the first phalanx is long and wide, it indicates sadness and superstition.
- The second phalanx, in gnarled fingers, indicates a passion for agriculture and for the exact sciences; in smooth fingers, aptitude for hidden magic.
- The long third knuckle indicates avarice.

## Ring finger: Fire finger

- The longer first phalanx indicates a passion for art.
- The long second phalanx also indicates logic and reason in art, and a just desire to get into the business sector.

- The third most developed phalanx indicates vanity, the desire to shine and to acquire wealth.

## Little finger: Air finger

- The first phalanx, if long, indicates a love of science, ease of speech.
- The second, more developed phalanx indicates a tendency towards industry, commerce and practical activities that require reasoning.
- The third phalanx indicates the material side, subterfuge, mischief up to the lie.

## Thumb: finger of the fifth element, Life.

In this finger, the root, i.e. the mount of Venus, is distinguished after the second phalanx and the first phalanx with the nail.
The highly developed root of the thumb (mount of Venus) indicates sensuality which can be dominated if the first phalanx, an indication of will, is long.

- If the thumb is particularly extended the will will be very strong because it will be based on logic, but it will not be tyrannical.
- If the thumb as a whole is of normal size, there will be a passive but very firm resistance.

The first phalanx, the one that carries the nail, represents the "will".

- If it is long and strong, it is a sign of powerful and energetic will and a lot of self-confidence.
- If the phalanx is very long and thick, the will will join the tyranny.

- If the phalanx is of medium length, there will be only passive resistance by force of inertia, equal mood, indecision.
- If the phalanx is short, it indicates an absolute lack of will, indifference, mood swings for no important reason.
- If the first phalanx is short and round, almost like a ball, it indicates ferocious instincts, a brutal character; likewise, if it is large and elongated with a short and flat nail, it confirms the brutal nature.
- If it is pointed, it announces sensitivity and impulsiveness, while if it is conical, it indicates a lack of perseverance.

The second phalanx represents "logic".
- If it is longer than the first, it indicates weak will and also logic and reasoning, but indecision.
- If it is much longer it indicates ease of discouragement and great changeability of mood.
- If it is of equal length compared to the first phalanx it means that logic and will are in equal measure and determine balance.

In addition to their meaning based on the shape, the phalanxes also represent the zodiac signs, each culture puts its own symbols and meanings by linking them to this or that other zodiac sign, for this reason it would also be important to be able to understand the cultural affiliation of the consultant, to get a more complete reading.

**The nails**

In the hands we can see the most varied forms of fingers and nails which serve to protect the end of the third phalanx.

- The nails, formed of a horny substance, have the task of protecting the extremely thin and sensitive nerve filaments which, through the epidermis, gather in the fingertips and are used for touch.

The formal nail must not be fragile, it must have a pale pink color and measure in the part adhering to the flesh as much as the part of the third phalanx that reaches the root of the nail from the beginning.

- The shape of the nails reveals indications of the subject's character.

If the nails are thin they denote finesse of touch and intellect, the thick and thick nails reveal lack of delicacy in the sense of touch, limited intellectual faculties and little perspicacity.
Hard nails indicate an energetic and decisive character while soft nails announce a soft nature and an indecisive character.
People who are imaginative and highly impressionable generally have long, arched nails.
Short nails denote a critical and positive spirit, acuity in judgments, readiness and love for discussions.
Flat nails, widened at the top of the fingers, if they are thick and hard, indicate a great propensity for movement and action, roughness, restlessness, a spirit of contradiction and a desire to fight and discuss.
Nails that are flat and wide but thin and transparent also indicate a need for activity, but only spiritual rather than physical and if

they also indicate a will to fight it is rather a search for intellectual struggle that allows one to support one's opinions and exercise a critical spirit .

The narrow, convex and pointed nails generally belong to tapered fingers; the subjects are then impressionable natures, not very perceptive and inconstant.

If the nails are hard, in addition to the lack of perspicacity one adds susceptibility and excessive self-respect, ease to envy and jealousy. Narrow, curved and delicate nails are for dreamers, sensitive creatures, often prone to melancholy.

- Short nails: tendency to bowel disease.
- Short and flat nails: predisposition to nervous diseases and brain disorders.
- Short, broad and brittle nails: disposition to paralysis.
- Thin and narrow nails - delicate health.
- Long nails - mediocre physical strength and poor health.
- Long nails widened at the top and bluish at the root: an indication of poor blood circulation, weak heart and nervous disorders.
- Nails without a white crescent on the underside and short and small: indicate a tendency to heart trouble; if the crescent is highly developed it indicates that blood circulation is good.
- Brittle, pale nails: weakness.
- Hard nails - good health.
- Nails curved at the apex on the finger: predisposition to chest diseases.
- Convex nails: disposition to diseases of the spinal cord.
- Yellowish nails: tendency to liver disease.
- Purple nails: poor health.
- Very colored or too pale nails: lymphatic nature and weakness.

When small white spots appear it is a sign of a nervous state in a sensitive temperament; they could also announce propitious events, while if the spots are black they should indicate the possibility of fatal events.

Congenital syphilis is revealed by small, thin, brittle, uneven and stained nails.

If the nails, especially of the thumb and forefinger, tend to curve as if they were entering the flesh, it is a sign of lung disorders; already the great doctor of antiquity, Hippocrates, observed that this type of nail is more easily noticed in young women, especially in blond types with delicate skin, and the greater or lesser curvature of the nail reflects the greater or lesser severity of the disease.

Fingernails furrowed lengthwise indicate excess of mental work and old age, while if they are furrowed lengthwise they are symptoms of acute illness and generally form after a few days from the onset of the disease.

It is advisable to observe the way in which the nails are kept because if they are badly kept or gnawed they indicate that the individual is a messy, distracted and rough type; on the contrary, nails kept in an accurate way, without refinement, are of active, sober and constant people.